Kevin Mackay's Greatest Corvette Finds

THE CORVETTE HUNTER

Tyler Greenblatt

CarTech®

CarTech®, Inc.
838 Lake Street South
Forest Lake, MN 55025
Phone: 651-277-1200 or 800-551-4754
Fax: 651-277-1203
www.cartechbooks.com

Edit by Wes Eisenschenk
Layout by Connie DeFlorin
Cover photo by Dave Wendt
Frontispiece photo by Bill Erdman

ISBN 978-1-61325-347-2
Item No. CT599

Library of Congress Cataloging-in-Publication Data

Names: Greenblatt, Tyler, author.
Title: The Corvette hunter : Kevin Mackay's greatest Corvette finds / Tyler Greenblatt.
Description: Forest Lake, MN : CarTech Books, [2018]
Identifiers: LCCN 2017042378 | ISBN 9781613253472
Subjects: LCSH: Corvette automobile. | Corvette automobile--History. | Automobiles--United States--History.
Classification: LCC TL215.C6 G74 2018 | DDC 629.222/2--dc23
LC record available at https://lccn.loc.gov/2017042378

Written, edited, and designed in the U.S.A.
Printed in China
10 9 8 7 6 5 4 3 2 1

DISTRIBUTION BY:

Europe
PGUK
63 Hatton Garden
London EC1N 8LE, England
Phone: 020 7061 1980 • Fax: 020 7242 3725
www.pguk.co.uk

Australia
Renniks Publications Ltd.
3/37-39 Green Street
Banksmeadow, NSW 2109, Australia
Phone: 2 9695 7055 • Fax: 2 9695 7355
www.renniks.com

Canada
Login Canada
300 Saulteaux Crescent
Winnipeg, MB, R3J-3T2 Canada
Phone: 800 665 1148 • Fax: 800 665 0103
www.lb.ca

CONTENTS

Acknowledgments

Tyler's Acknowledgments

I'd like to thank my wife, Danielle, for not leaving me years ago when I bought a Corvette instead of an engagement ring. But I especially thank her for finally agreeing to ride in it . . . and then finally agreeing to marry me once I corrected that mistake.

I thank my parents, for being cool enough to own a Corvette while living in Manhattan and for having me when you could still throw a kid in the back of a Sting Ray (with a bolted down seat and seat belt that Kevin installed for them). I also admit that I should have learned from my father, who was smart enough to buy my mom the Corvette as a wedding present after they got married, even though I've only ever seen her drive it twice.

Thank you to Kevin Mackay, for not only hooking me on Corvettes while I was still in a car seat but for continuing to foster my love for America's Sports Car simply by living his own passion. He has inspired me with his work ethic, positive attitude in the wake of major setbacks, and care for others—all attributes that extend well beyond cars. He gave up many hours to participate in this project and never once did he not answer my phone call or take the time to thoroughly tell his many Corvette stories.

Thank you to Wes Eisenschenk, and the entire staff at CarTech, for allowing Kevin and myself to tell these stories in a way that goes well beyond the cars and the nuts and bolts of a restoration. Most of these stories have never been told publically and certainly not to the extent that we've done here.

Kevin's Acknowledgments

The following individuals need to be acknowledged because of their guidance, support, and friendship. I wouldn't be here today if it wasn't for them.

My father, Jeremiah, who tried to keep me on the right path at all times and who taught me right from wrong, to have a never-give-up attitude, and to work with others. In the beginning, he thought I would never make it as a grease monkey. I had to prove him wrong. I just wanted to follow my dream, and the last nine years of his life he worked at my shop. I got to know him as a loving father who only wanted the best for his family.

Bill Linkner, my wrestling coach. Between my father and my wrestling coach, I feared him the most. I was a wild and crazy kid, and if it wasn't for me getting involved in wrestling who knows what would've happened to me. He kept me out of a lot of trouble. Coach Linkner kept me focused, driven, and off the streets. We had one of the best wrestling programs in New York State back then. Even today we have a great relationship. He owns a very original 1958 Corvette and has a room full of trophies to prove it.

David Burroughs, the founder of Bloomington Gold, took me under his wing when he wrote the book *Corvette Restoration, State of the Art* on a 1965 396 COPO-ordered car. I read that book many times over and it made a very big impact on me from the very beginning. I finally tracked him down to talk about my restoration, and every question that I asked he would have an answer. That was tremendous for me because I was just starting out and he really took the time and had a lot of patience with me. He told me that if I was going to Bloomington for the first time that I would be lucky to get a Silver. I told him I wasn't going unless I get a Gold, that's why I was talking to him. I was just starting out, he didn't know who I was, but he took the time and groomed me to who I am today. After I got the Gold with the highest percentage in my class, I decided to become a judge. I'm now going into my 34th year as a Bloomington Gold judge.

Ed Mueller, the number one Corvette collector back in the 1980s. I met him at the Malcolm Konner show and he was so impressed with the work I did that when I first opened my shop, he became one of my first customers. He believed in me and groomed me to go after the best of the best Corvettes.

Chip Miller was one of the cofounders of Carlisle Events and the most respected person in the Corvette hobby. Everybody loved him. I learned so much from him and spoke to him daily for many years. He gave me insight on true car collecting, and he just loved the hobby. He was one of the worst guys to go to a swap meet with because he would talk to everybody and it would take forever to walk around.

Lance Miller is a chip off the old block. Chip would be very proud of his son. Lance took the lead after his father's passing and completed his dad's dream of bringing the number three Le Mans racer, which we found, back to Le Mans 50 years later with the only surviving driver, John Fitch. Please check out the documentary *The Quest.* I see so much of his dad in him. Thank you for what you do for me and for your friendship.

Phil Schwartz was also one of my first customers. Phil has been into cars since the time he could drive one. After doing well in school, his dad bought him a 1969 Baldwin-Motion Corvette with all the bells and whistles, but when it came time to starting a family, the Corvette had to go. He spoke about this car for 25 years. You can read the whole story in this book. He became a great friend and he was there from the beginning.

Angelo Castelli was one of my first customers and has been a trusting friend and business consultant for more than 30 years, going back to the winter of 1985 when I was renting a one-bay garage and starting my business. He has been Corvette Repair's marketing and advertising director and is responsible for maintaining the website and handling advertising and promotional campaigns. Thank you for watching my back and being there for me.

Irwin Kroiz, you are truly a gentleman and a 100-percent class act. I have the most respect for you, my dear friend. We think alike and eat alike. I have some wonderful times and many laughs with you. We travel together to most of the big shows and always have laughs. You've given me some great advice over the years and I want to tell you thank you for your friendship.

Franz Estereicher, who I met at Corvettes at Carlisle 18 years ago. He's a super nice person and is known in the Corvette hobby as the "Keeper of Knowledge." He's a very private and humble individual and I was honored to be invited to his beautiful home, where he welcomed me with open arms and shared his collection of documents. I was blown away. Franz is a researcher's researcher who always helps me when I'm in need. He always dots his i's and crosses his t's. A rare breed indeed. Please keep up the fine work, my dear friend.

Bryan Shook, you are my guardian angel. You came to my rescue when I was in need. We were glued at the hip for those 2-1/2 years. We could write a book about it, which I know would be a bestseller. You truly know what you're doing and have the passion and drive to succeed. Thank you for watching my back. How can I not like you? We have the same birthday.

Without my team at Corvette Repair this never would've happened. We have been so fortunate to have worked on the most desirable, rarest, best-of-the-best Corvettes, and they just keep coming in. If the walls could talk the history that would come out of them would be unbelievable. I'll always say this: you are only as good as your team, and as a team we're unbeatable. Thank you guys.

To Christina, my first wife, my first love, and who, for many years, was a Corvette widow. We were just kids when we fell in love. You were the first girl I kissed, the first girl whose hand I held, and the first girl I went on a date with. I still remember that first date; we went fishing. I'm so happy that you came back into my life after all those years; you always held a special place in my heart. And I'm not done with you, yet.

Foreword

by Reggie Jackson

There are a handful of Corvette guys out there who are considered the biggest and most knowledgeable when it comes to the buying, selling, restoring, and preserving of important Corvettes. But when it comes to the real high-end cars, the number one guy is Kevin Mackay. Kevin's credibility, honesty, character, and knowledge is unmatched when it comes to collectible 1953 to 1972 Corvettes.

I met Kevin in 2007 at Barrett-Jackson when a mutual friend of ours, Joe Calcagno, pointed him out up on stage. I went up to him and his fiancée (at the time), Christina, and told him that I was a big fan of his and that I'd love to talk Corvettes with him. The next year, I saw him again at Bloomington Gold, where he asked if I'd like to drive his see-through L88. Of course I took him up on it. The car has no covers on the sidepipes because it's meant for competition, and I got a second-degree burn on my leg stepping out of it! But it was not a bad memory at all, in fact, I don't have any bad memories in the car world. Six months later, I did the same thing getting out of my competition 427 Cobra.

The biggest mistake that Kevin ever made was when I owed him $600. I finally saw him at Pebble Beach after a few years of owing him money, counted $600 out of my wallet, and handed it to him. It was funny, we made a big deal out of it, and he was happy. But afterward, I think he regretted collecting the money because the story of me owing him money was worth more to him than getting the money. Looking back, if he could do it over again, I think he would turn it down just for the fun of it.

The Corvette hobby is a small world, it's an exciting world, and what makes it exciting with Kevin is that he knows where all the good stuff is and who's got it. On his worst day, he's one of the top guys in the hobby, if not the top guy. Kevin's knowledge of individual components, numbers, stampings, and originality is incredible. He covers every aspect of restoring a Corvette from the beauty and presentation, to fit and finish, to the mechanicals and engine. He can look at a car, know its current value, where it should be, and how to get it there. There are a few guys in his class, but I think, objectively, that Kevin has the most all-around knowledge in the Corvette hobby. You might say that Kevin Mackay is the Mr. October of Corvettes.

I have three cars that Kevin has blessed: a 9,600-mile '65 white on red leather coupe that's untouched, unrestored, featured in the Bloomington Gold Great Hall, and achieved an NCRS Five-Star Bowtie award; a '67 silver with black stinger car famously nicknamed 007 because those are the last three digits on the serial number; and another '67 Marina Blue on blue car. I've enjoyed Kevin coming into my shop and telling me that these cars are the real deal. It makes me feel good as a collector and owner. Kevin has told me to stay away from a couple cars, too. He's saved me a lot of money and heartache.

Being in the collector car hobby, I just enjoy being around people who have the knowledge that Kevin does. I've had an interest in cars since I was a child and being around guys who teach me and let me learn is fun for me. Knowledge is worth money. It's valuable. Getting that knowledge from the best out there, not only Kevin, but the others on the top as well, is extremely valuable. Kevin's a special guy, he's a special guy to the hobby, and I'm glad he's my friend.

Introduction

Kevin Mackay officially opened Corvette Repair in 1985, renting a one-bay garage out of an auto repair shop in Valley Stream, New York. He didn't know back then that there would soon be a need for high-end Corvette restorations and maintenance work. After receiving widespread praise for his first restoration, a 1965 Corvette coupe, he realized he had the talent to achieve award-winning results. In 1987, a new custom-built facility was officially opened where it currently sits today. It has been expanded over the years to meet the varying needs of scrupulous Corvette owners and collectors. Over the last 30 years, Kevin and his team of specialists have earned a world-class reputation for restoring many of the finest and most famous Corvettes to ever see the street or the track. Many have even been secret experimental cars hand-built by the father of Corvette himself, Zora Arkus-Duntov.

Today, Kevin's passion and knowledge are unmatched in the Corvette hobby. Since its inception, Corvette Repair has been awarded 517 NCRS Top Flights, 198 Bloomington Gold awards, 139 Bloomington Gold Special Collection awards, 137 Triple Crown Diamond awards, 5 Bloomington Gold Great Hall awards, 113 Carlisle Chip's Choice invitations, 21 NCRS Duntov awards, 28 Bloomington Gold Hall of Fame awards, 22 Bloomington Gold Benchmark awards, and 20 NCRS American Heritage awards. In addition to winning awards, Kevin is an NCRS Master Judge and Bloomington Gold Benchmark Judge. Corvettes restored by Corvette Repair have also won awards at such high-profile events as the Pebble Beach Concours d'Elegance and the Amelia Island Concours d'Elegance.

In 2010, the documentary, *The Quest,* was released, featuring Kevin as one of the principal narration speakers. Produced by filmmaker Michael Brown, the story followed Kevin and friend Lance Miller's quest to return the legendary 1960 Briggs Cunningham #3 Corvette, which won its class at Le Mans in Corvette's first attempt there, back to France for the 50th anniversary of its win.

In June 2012, Kevin was awarded one of the highest honors in the Corvette hobby by being inducted into the Great Hall, which consists of 50 individuals who have done incredible work to improve the Corvette and the hobby. In 2014, he was invited to be the Grand Marshall of the Corvette Homecoming in Bowling Green, Kentucky.

Along with that invitation came the additional honor of being made an official Kentucky Colonel.

Kevin has been featured in numerous publications and is often spotted on television at auctions and giving interviews at car shows. He continues to take part in elite discussion panels and Q & A sessions at automotive events worldwide, and he teaches classes and seminars about classic Corvettes and their restoration. Although his work has been seen on more than 100 magazine covers and in numerous books and television shows, this is the first book entirely devoted to his life's work and his unmatched passion for Corvette.

Publisher's Note: In reporting history, the images required to tell the tale will vary greatly in quality, especially by modern photographic standards. While some images in this volume are not up to those digital standards, we have included them, as we feel they are an important element in telling the story.

CHAPTER 1

The Beginning

HOW KEVIN MACKAY BECAME THE CORVETTE HUNTER

In 1981, Kevin Mackay purchased a 1965 Nassau Blue small-block Corvette coupe with the money he earned from selling his '64 convertible. The 64,000-mile car was nearly complete and original, and would make an excellent starting point for a restoration. Living with his parents and working as a mechanic for the city of New York, he parked his new Corvette in the backyard and drove his parents' station wagon to work. Even though he could have easily fixed up the Corvette and drove it, he wanted to give the car a 100-percent-perfect restoration. As a single guy living with his parents, he had plenty of time to invest the hours in making his car the best Corvette he possibly could.

He created a master list of all the specific parts he needed and traveled the country attending swap meets until every last correctly identified bolt had been found. He even went so far as to source the correct new old stock (NOS) Firestone tires from a man in Georgia who shipped them to him in Long Island. Because he was working on the project in a greenhouse in his parents' backyard, Kevin had to outsource the paintwork, which he oversaw to his exacting specifications.

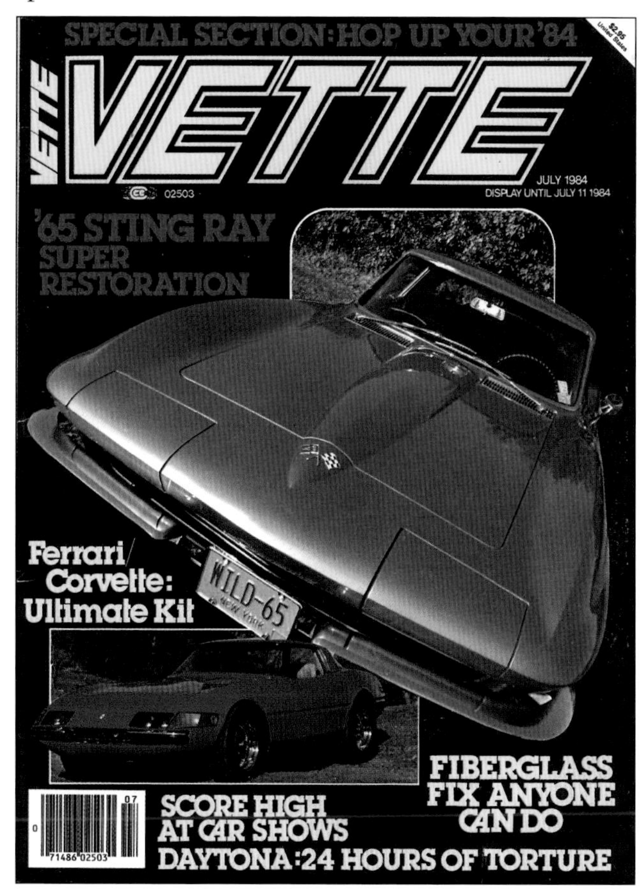

The July 1984 issue of Vette *magazine featured the first of many Corvettes restored by Kevin and his team at Corvette Repair.* Wild '65 *was the car that really got things started for him not only on the show circuit but also with Corvette enthusiasts everywhere thanks to the* Vette *feature.*

Kevin's first shop, called "Corvette Repairs" instead of "Corvette Repair" consisted of a rented one-car garage not too far from the current facility. It sure beat working in his parents' backyard.

One of the many times that Kevin and "Father of the Corvette" Zora Arkus-Duntov crossed paths.

It took him two years to complete the car, spending every minute working on it when he was not repairing trucks for the city. Finally, he finished the car to a high enough standard that the next thing to do was take it to one of the New York and New Jersey area's largest Corvette shows, held annually at Malcolm Konner Chevrolet in New Jersey. But not before the car received its finishing touch: a vanity license plate that read "WILD-65." The entries were judged by various experts and oftentimes Corvette Chief Engineer Zora Arkus-Duntov was in attendance.

Kevin parked the Nassau Blue 4-speed coupe in its place and waited for the judging to begin. Sure enough, Arkus-Duntov was there along with GM Chief of Design Larry Shinoda. While Kevin was taking it all in, one of the judges approached to ask about the car. He introduced himself as Ed Mueller. Kevin recognized his name immediately from the many car magazines that featured his collection. "Young man," Mueller said to Kevin, who was in his early 20s at the time, "this is a very beautiful car. What shop did the work?"

"I did the car myself," Kevin told him. Mueller was incredulous that not only did Kevin do the work himself but he did it at home and not in a professional restoration shop. Mueller handed Kevin his business card.

"If you ever open up your own business, I want to be your customer," he told Kevin as he handed over the card. "I'm very impressed with your work." Kevin was flattered by the compliment from one of the best-known collectors of the day.

The day got better. Kevin's coupe was chosen, out of the 100 cars present, as Best In Show. "I was in tears," he remembers. "I was so emotionally overwhelmed that out of all the cars that were there, they picked mine as the best car in the whole show. Here's a guy who built this out of his parents' backyard."

Three years later, one of the best blessings in disguise happened to Kevin, who continued to drive and enjoy his coupe. He got laid off from his job with the city. His first instinct was to go back to the Chevrolet dealership, where he had previously worked, or one of the other area dealerships that was hiring mechanics. But, although he loved working on all cars, his real passion was Corvettes. He had been doing work on local Corvettes out of his parents' house, and the amount of work continued to increase. He decided that instead of seeking another job he would open his own shop and only work on Corvettes. The name would be simple, to the point, and effective: Corvette Repair.

At first, the startup took the form of a rented one-bay garage near his home in Valley Stream, New York. The year was 1985, and Kevin needed to show off his work at the national level, so he took his Nassau Blue coupe to the Bloomington meet, where it was certified Gold, scoring the highest number of points awarded to a '65 that year. It was the first Gold of many.

Back at the small one-bay garage known as Corvette Repair, Kevin remembered Mueller telling him years ago that he would be his customer if he ever opened his own shop. With Mueller's business card still handy, he called him. "I don't know if you remember me," Kevin began. "My name is Kevin Mackay."

Mueller did remember him. "Oh, wait a minute, you're that young kid I met years ago. How are you doing?"

"Well, I'm not doing too good. I lost my job, so I started my own Corvette business. I could sure use some work." Mueller provided just that in the form of a car that needed some freshening. It was his yellow 1969 ZL1, one of two built and one of the rarest Corvettes on the planet. The car had been restored professionally, but Mueller thought that a couple of things could be perfected and that Kevin was the man to do it. Kevin did a little paintwork on the car followed by a concours-level detail job throughout the entire car.

"When I shipped the car back to him I was nervous," Kevin remembers. "I hoped he would like it; I put my heart and soul into that car. And he went crazy over it." Mueller was so impressed with the workmanship that he couldn't wait to send the next car out to Long Island.

Every time Kevin finished a car and sent it back, Ed Mueller said, "I have another one for you."

"This went on for 17 years in a row. He's one of the guys who put me on the map. Everyone knew who Ed Mueller was and that I was working for him."

With their working relationship quickly turning into a mentorship and friendship, the two spoke candidly on the phone one day. "Kevin, I'll never forget when I met you," Mueller started. "I met you at the Malcolm Konner Chevrolet show and I didn't want to tell you this then because I didn't know you, but I'm going to tell you now because I consider you like a son to me." He paused. "I think you're an ***hole."

Kevin wasn't sure he had heard him correctly. He did.

"You're an ***hole, but I love you, and I'm going to tell you why you're an ***hole. You're doing the wrong kind of cars."

"What do you mean?" Kevin asked, taken aback as to why a man who had just complimented him was insulting him. "I'm doing Corvettes; what do you mean I'm working on the wrong cars?"

"Listen to me, Kevin, and you'll understand. Whether it's a big-block Corvette or a small-block Corvette or a Tanker or a ZL1, all these cars are basically the same. They have the same bodies, same interiors, same chassis, and the only major difference is the engine."

Kevin couldn't disagree with that. He had worked on enough of them to know what Mueller was talking about.

"So you have that 300-horse car that you did," Mueller continued, "which is really a gorgeous car; the only problem is there's not any value on it. Now if this car were a 396, or a '67 435-horse car, it would be worth double or triple the amount of money. Same body, same interior, same chassis; it's just the engine that's different. Now if you put all your heart and soul and your passion and talent into a rarer or more desirable car, you'd be better off. Your car wasn't worth restoring. It's a great car, a great driver and starter, but you've got to take it to a different level."

Kevin understood completely what Ed Mueller was telling him. The next car he bought for himself was a black-on-red '67 427/435 coupe in March 1988. The options were incredible and Kevin later discovered that car was the legendary *Bounty Hunter*. He treated it to a complete frame-off restoration and, although he desperately wanted to keep it for himself, he had a financial partner in his growing business who didn't share his vision and passion for the brand. In 1991, Kevin had had enough and decided to sell the car. Ed Mueller immediately stepped up to buy it and handed Kevin $100,000 in cash. "Now you're getting smart," he said. It was enough money to finish buying out his partner and lead Corvette Repair on his own.

When he wasn't working at the shop, which wasn't often, Kevin was at home thumbing through old magazines. He started to become interested in what he considered to be the greatest Corvette option package ever made. He had quickly outgrown even '67 Tri-Power cars and wanted to step up to the baddest of the bad: RPO L88. However, he couldn't even come close to being able to afford one.

He continued to look through the old magazines, admiring the famous L88 race cars that duked it out at Sebring, Daytona, and even Le Mans when it hit him. He had never seen or heard of most of these cars in present times. Of course the Grand Sports were known, as were some of the more famous race cars that had major class wins and continued to be used at showcase events through the years. Cars such as Roger Penske's '66 Sunoco Blue coupe that won back-to-back at Sebring and Daytona. But there were other class-winning factory L88s that had much success and were never seen again. So what if they were sitting in a junkyard somewhere with the engine missing? A factory L88 race car is still a factory L88 and could be restored as such just as easily as any other Corvette.

"I realized that there were a lot of those cars out there that had never been found. The official publication of Corvette is *Corvette News*, and I thought that any car featured on the cover would have to be something important. A lot of them were factory L88s that won championships. I decided to go after all of them.

"Some people started to get jealous. They'd say, 'How can one guy find all these rare cars?' You know how? When you don't have a life, like me; that's how you find these cars. My whole life I was just obsessed with the history of these cars and finding out where the hell they were. While others were on vacation or at home with their families watching a movie, you know what I was doing? I was looking through a telephone book or at the classified ads in an old magazine. I was studying photos in old books, making connections, and getting phone numbers. That's what I was doing in my spare time. I'd sleep for six or seven hours, and the rest of the time I'd be hunting, restoring, working, repairing; whatever I had to do. So that's how I found these cars. Other guys were at home. There's nothing wrong with that; family is as important as anything, but at the time I wasn't married, I was living on my own, I was independent, so my whole life was Corvettes. That's why I got this stuff, because I had the drive and the will and the passion to do it.

"I went down a lot of dead-end streets. Not everything was a pot of gold. A lot of cars turned up stolen, destroyed, or burned to the ground. But that's the way it is."

As he started finding some of these long-lost race cars through perseverance and gut-bending willpower, he continued to learn from Ed Mueller about the investment side of the car hobby. He was brought in the loop of other well-known collectors including Chip Miller, founder of Corvettes at Carlisle, who also took Kevin under his wing and groomed him into one of the top Corvette experts in the world. Kevin's first major Corvette sale in 2000 took three cars out of his garage and put $1 million into his bank account. He could have retired on the interest; instead, he spent all of it on his dream Corvette.

Even as the cost of some restorations at Corvette Repair neared half a million dollars, and the awards continued to pile up more than any other Corvette shop in history, the featured magazine covers exceeded 100, and Kevin Mackay took on celebrity-like status on television and at car events worldwide, he never lost the drive to hunt down long-lost Corvettes.

"I like the challenge, I like the hunt, and I love the history. It's fun. Life is short; we're only caretakers of these special cars, but as long as I've got my health I'll keep plugging away. That's what keeps me happy. I didn't take my first vacation until I was 50 because I got married when I was 50."

With hardly any time available to date, how did he meet someone, fall in love, and get married? In ninth grade, Kevin started dating Christina, and the two quickly fell in love. From their first date when Kevin took her fishing to learning how to drive together in driver's ed, they knew they were meant for each other. When Kevin turned 16, she gave him a seashell engraved with the words: Kevin And Christina, Love You Forever, 7/12/1973. The pair shared two years together, sharing first dates, first handholds, and first kisses.

Kevin was the captain of his Junior High wrestling team and his coach, who was incidentally his and Christina's driving instructor, told him that he couldn't have any relationships; it would screw with his head. So Kevin broke up with Christina. She was devastated.

Fast forward 30 years when Kevin received an invitation to his 30th high school reunion and, of course, went online to see who else had signed up to attend. He saw a familiar name: Christina Cantone. He couldn't believe it. All the memories of his first love came back in a whirlwind rush. He had to contact her before the reunion, so he sent an email with the heading "Your First Love." He said that he was looking forward to seeing her and he hoped that all was well. She responded, signing her email "Your First Love." Sixty emails later, Christina called Corvette Repair and Kevin recognized her voice immediately. She asked how many kids Kevin had, to which he responded, "I was never married, I have no children, and I'm not gay."

"I have no kids, I'm divorced, and I'm not gay either," she said. After they shared a good laugh, Kevin mentioned that he would be in West Palm Beach, Florida, the following week, near where Christina lived, for the Barrett-Jackson auction. She invited him to stay at her house. She told him that she had been so in love with him when she was a kid and that she had never gotten over him.

He had never gotten over her either. That night, he went into his attic and opened a box containing every love letter she had ever written to him and the old seashell that she had inscribed with a rusty nail in her father's garage. He flew to West Palm Beach, and Christina was there at the airport waiting for him.

"She had this beautiful tan and looked great," Kevin remembers. "She had put on makeup and jewelry and a beautiful outfit. She never looked like that in high school! I was used to seeing her in jeans and a T-shirt."

Christina ran up to him and hugged him and kissed him. They walked over to the baggage claim and Kevin said, "Do me a favor and hold on to this," as he placed the seashell in her hand. Tears ran down her face. She couldn't believe that he had saved the seashell from more than 30 years ago. He told her that she was his first love and she had always held a place in his heart. That night they went out for dinner, drinks, and dancing, and Kevin had another special surprise waiting for her at home.

"I'm not done with you just yet," he told her. He then pulled out a binder containing every love letter she had ever written him, in order by date. A year and a half later, Kevin proposed, they got married, and he went on his first vacation that didn't involve Corvettes.

It seemed as though Kevin Mackay was getting everything that he could have possibly dreamed of: a successful business, a loving wife, and the ability to pursue his Corvette passion every single day. And despite all the magazine articles written about his work and the television and event interviews he's been a part of, he's never truly been able to tell the stories behind the cars to his fans. Some of his greatest finds have been the result of years, sometimes decades, of persistent grit and cunning.

"I may have been interviewed about the cars I've restored, but they don't know about what I had to go through to get them. They may see the cars done now and they're all beautiful and pretty, but they don't know what it took to get there. That's why this book is so important. Readers are going to say 'Holy crap! This guy is out of his freaking mind. This guy never gives up!' When I do something I try to go all out at any given time and I don't give up. Maybe that's just my nature. I have a high school education and although I'm not a good reader or a good speller, I have the drive and I have the will and I have the passion."

Christmas 1962 was a special time for a seven-year-old Kevin Mackay. He received a toy Indy race car as a gift! Even then, although he loved tractors, trucks, and trains like most boys, he especially loved race cars. His sister, Colleen is standing up with her doll right behind his brother, Jerry. Kevin's other brother, Brian, experienced his first Christmas that year.

After winning a local soap box derby race, Kevin (right) poses with his brother Jerry and their impressive trophy.

Kevin and his wife, Christina.

CHAPTER 2

1967 427/435 Coupe

BOUNTY HUNTER

In 1967, Vernon Turner, a salesman at Krieger's Chevrolet in Woodridge, New York, ordered a 435-hp big-block coupe in the incredibly rare combination of black exterior and red interior. It's now known to be one of four coupes so ordered, in addition to two black-with-red convertibles. The signature red stinger hood stripe and redline tires accented the car's appearance beautifully. As a demo car, Turner drove it to work every day, but he also drag raced it on the weekends. A big fan of famous drag racer Connie Kalitta, who named his cars *Bounty Hunter,* Turner did likewise and applied "Bounty Hunter" decals to the fenders and installed black Cragar GT aluminum mag wheels. He also installed a CB radio, which meant mounting a second antenna to the rear of the car.

After six months, Turner sold the car. He was killed just a short time later in what is believed to be a mob hit. It has been alleged that the car was also used to run drugs and guns across state lines and shows up in several FBI stakeout videos and images.

The *Bounty Hunter* Corvette then went through 17 different owners and saw much of the typical 1970s and 1980s customization on its journey. It had fender flares grafted on, Motion Performance did some work on the car, and at one point it was even painted green with purple snakes all over it. It was fish-scale brown at another point in its life and had a variety of different wheels. By the early 1980s, it was typical Corvette red but retained its diamond-tufted interior, likely from its purple snake days. Like so many great cars during that time, its rare showroom form and interesting history had been left long behind.

The Find

In March 1988, Kevin received a call from Alan Kaplan saying that he had a line on a factory black big-block coupe with red interior. He said that he'd turn Kevin on to the car, and Kevin would pay him a $500 broker fee if he bought it. That was a fair tradeoff, and Kaplan told Kevin about an ad in *Vette Vues* magazine for the car, which was owned by Terry Golden.

Kevin went to see the car and ascertain its original setup because the car had by then been painted, customized, and was running headers and mag wheels. He opened the gas cap, removed the rubber boot, and shined his flashlight into the tank itself to read the original tank sticker, which was still glued in place. The car checked all the boxes: Tuxedo Black paint, red vinyl trim, 435 Turbo-Jet engine, 4:11 rear end, factory sidepipes, power steering, power brakes, power windows,

Kevin and his team at Corvette Repair restored the 1967 big-block coupe to the way Vernon Turner owned it with the* Bounty Hunter *decals on the fenders and the Cragar GT aluminum mag wheels. In this condition, the car scored an NCRS Top Flight award, even with maximum points taken off for paint and aftermarket wheels. The car looks mean with the red stinger, red interior, and redline tires! (Photo Courtesy Bill Erdman)

and redline tires.

At the time, Kevin had never heard of another black/red 435 coupe. In fact, this car was the only known, documented one in existence. "The car had amazing options," he says. "The codes were very important to me, and black happens to be my favorite color. Knowing that black is the rarest color for that year (they only made 815 black cars), how many are 435s? How many have all the special options?"

With the goal of buying and restoring an extra-special car to the highest possible caliber, Kevin had been saving every cent he made, waiting for the right opportunity to come along. "A black and red 435 coupe with sidepipes; you can't get much better than that," he says. "So I purchased the car for $19,600 and couldn't get the money out fast enough!"

While undertaking the initial restoration, which saw the body and chassis restored separately, Kevin hired private investigator David Reisner to track down the history of the unique car. "Somebody had to order this car special because of all these options," he points out. "You don't get all these options on a 435 car, especially power steering and all the goodies on it."

Reisner traced the car back through 17 owners, with the original dealership already being known due to the dealer zone number on the gas tank sticker. Reisner even found a few old black and white photographs of the car on the dealership floor in its *Bounty Hunter* trim.

"We gotta restore the car just the way it is on the showroom floor," Kevin says. "What a great piece of history!"

Life As a Driveable Chassis

The Corvette Repair crew did an initial body-on restoration of *Bounty Hunter,* which included the removal of the fender flares and the addition of a complete New Old Stock (NOS) GM nose. Kevin brought it out for its first public appearance at the 1988 National Corvette Restorers Society (NCRS) National Convention. The event had a drag racing portion held at Maple Grove Raceway, and because the car started life as a drag racer, it made the perfect setting for its launch into the limelight.

Kevin's longtime friend, customer, and mentor Ed Mueller showed up with Grand Sport #2, which he had just purchased for $800,000. Kevin estimates that car's value at nearly $10 million today. "So I'm

The Bounty Hunter *Corvette has no clothes! While it may not look like much to most people, the Tri-Power air cleaner and sidepipes hint that this car is something special. Take note of the valve cover signed by Zora Arkus-Duntov as well as "Zora" written on the frame by Kevin's knee.*

You didn't think the drivable chassis was just for show, did you? Here's Kevin ripping down the street by Corvette Repair. One can only imagine the incredible sound emanating from those sidepipes!

seeing all these cars racing down the dragstrip, and I wanted to take this car and race against the Grand Sport," Kevin says. "I was egging Ed on: 'Let's see that ****box Grand Sport you just purchased; let's go drag race!' He said, 'Kevin, I don't want to embarrass you; this car's got half the weight, but if you want to race, you're on!'

"So we go down the dragstrip and what does he do? He blows right by me, I hit a patch of antifreeze, and I punch the car right into the guardrail. The car starts smoking in the front; people thought it was on fire. I was so embarrassed that I crashed the car going in a straight line that I had my head down against the steering wheel. We just put this brand-new GM NOS nose on the car that cost me a small fortune. People were yelling, 'Get out of the car!' I said, 'I'm not getting out of the car, I'm too embarrassed. I can't believe I crashed this damn car.'

"Eventually they had to pull me out because they thought it was on fire. What happened was, when I hit the guardrail, the lower hose fell off the car and all this hot steam's coming out of it. People thought it was actual smoke from a fire."

Kevin was bestowed a special award that year for crashing the car, since the *Bounty Hunter* versus Grand Sport race had drawn a massive crowd of spectators. As Kevin likes to remember it: "I crashed it going against one of the greatest Corvettes in history."

Because the car needed a major rebuild after the accident, the Corvette Repair crew this time separated the body from the chassis and initiated a total, painstaking restoration on each component individually.

Kevin's father, who worked for the *New York Times* for 32 years, told him early on in his business, "Kevin, you gotta come up with a niche. You have to do something that's never been done."

What could Kevin bring to the Corvette hobby, and the automotive world, that no one had seen before? How could he leave his mark while taking his business to a whole new level that he had only dreamed of? Unforeseen as the great idea his father had urged him to deliver, Kevin began taking the restored rolling chassis to local shows. It garnered plenty of interest, as most people are only used to seeing the finished product of a restoration, even though "85 percent of the workmanship is underneath the car."

"I did that a couple of times, but I got tired of pushing that damn thing around. I wondered how much more I really had to do on it to make it driveable. Put a seat in it, put a master cylinder in it, some wiring, bumpers? That's exactly what we'll do, we'll make a driveable chassis."

A local Chevrolet dealership car show would be the place to gauge reactions to a driveable-chassis Corvette. Loving to give fellow car enthusiasts and spectators a show, Kevin unloaded the driveable chassis, which wasn't street legal, a block away from the dealership and proceeded to drive it at 40 mph back and forth past the show.

"The entire crowd left the show and watched me drive this creation up and down the highway for about eight or nine minutes. Then I finally drove into the show and the crowd was around that thing the whole time. I thought, 'You know, I think I got something here.' People were blown away. Not only was the craftsmanship excellent, everything was functional and driveable. So now we had something."

Kevin Mackay and his Corvette Repair shop was instantly on the map. They brought the driveable chassis to all the national shows, making it one of the most photographed cars in the 1980s. He continued to promote it, and fans continued to go crazy for it. "They heard about it, they read about it, they saw it. It's a win-win situation for all," he says. "It's good for me as the owner of the car, it's good for my business because of the exposure, and people get an education seeing the inner workings of a Corvette.

"My competitors didn't know where I came from. When I brought this thing to the national level, I brought it out exposed. It's like having a girl take her clothes off and walk down the beach. Everyone's going to look. If she had her clothes on, *eh,* they'd probably look at her if she's a cutie. Imagine being a cutie with no clothes on; you're going to get a lot more looks.

"I was really exposed with this chassis, so I had to make sure that whoever looked at this thing, I had to make a lasting impression on them, whether it was a potential customer or a guy wanting to learn what went where and how things mounted. But I really got off when I saw well-known restorers taking notes and taking photographs. I knew we had something there and I knew I had to take every creation to another level.

"I want to be the guy who pushes the envelope at all times. I thrive on the challenge, and I thrive on the competition. I'm a very bad sore loser. If I go there, I go there to win. I want to make sure that I'm very proud of what my staff and I have done and achieved. So I always push the envelope, and it's fun. To this day I haven't lost my drive. After 33 years, I still love doing it."

NCRS Top Flight Award

With *Bounty Hunter* finally put together again as a complete car, none other than Ed Mueller purchased it in 1991 for the record sale price of $100,000. The Corvette Repair team campaigned it for him, showing it in the Bloomington Gold Special Collection, Chip's Choice at Corvettes at Carlisle, and the Malcolm Konner Chevrolet Show. It took home a Bloomington Gold Award and an NCRS Top Flight Award.

The NCRS Top Flight Award proved to be somewhat of an undertaking by Kevin when he took the car to the regional meet in Cypress Gardens, Florida. *Bounty Hunter* was all done up in its special trim with the decals and the Cragar mag wheels. Kevin had the black and white photos of the car sitting in the showroom like that, and that's the way he felt he should restore the car. The Corvette's story was bigger than the car itself.

A couple of NCRS judges approached Kevin and the car on judging day and asked him what he wanted to do with the car. He responded that he wanted it judged for Flight. The judges were shocked. "You can't do that!" they said. "Look at the decals and the wheels."

"I understand it has the decals on the fenders and aftermarket wheels, but they're part of the car's story," Kevin responded.

"It's an insult to the NCRS!" the judges decried. "We can't judge this car."

Kevin was beginning to get annoyed at this point. He knew that the wheels and the decals would only lose him a few points on the otherwise pristine restoration that the Corvette Repair team had done. "Look," he said, "I'm a paying NCRS member, and I have all the documentation on the car and everything required for flight judging."

And so the judges went through the car and gave it near perfect points for the interior, chassis, and engine. When it came to the paint, they awarded no points. Kevin argued that every other panel on the car, the hood, roof, rear deck, quarter panels, everything else was perfect and that the decals were only on the fenders. The judges stood their ground and the car received zero points for paint, as well as a loss of points on the wheels, which Kevin had assumed.

That night at the awards banquet, Kevin was still fuming about the judging fiasco earlier. Many of his customers were in attendance, and it would hurt his reputation to enter a car and not win Top Flight. The judge who had given Kevin grief earlier that day went to the podium to announce the event's Top Flight winners. Sure enough, Kevin's name was called! Even with earning zero points on the paint, the rest of the car carried it over the 94-point threshold for Top Flight awards.

"They can only take off so many points for paint, and since everything else was perfect, the car still qualified!" Kevin says. "I threatened to paint flames on the car and bring it back the next year!"

"The car made such an impact in the hobby at the time that it was invited to go to the National Corvette Museum Annex," Kevin says. "We brought that car down with the '67 L88 Le Mans racer that Ed Mueller owned to show in the Annex, before the museum was built, to promote the future museum. They just wanted that thing down there, which was really cool. I was getting some really great PR with that car."

The only thing missing from the way Vernon Turner had the car set up is the CB radio. The 435 hp **Bounty Hunter** ***looks ready to pounce at a moment's notice. The "1967" license plate is a must for the non-Corvette people in the crowd, as any Corvette fan can tell a real '67 from the center-mount reverse lights and the five-slot side vents behind the front wheel. (Photo Courtesy Bill Erdman)***

Into the Future

Bounty Hunter is one of the small handful of Corvettes that Kevin had originally hoped never to sell, but he had to put his business first. The $100,000 sale to Ed Mueller didn't go toward buying new equipment or another special car, it went toward the actual purchase of Corvette Repair in the form of buying out his partner, whom Kevin was eager to remove.

"We sat down like gentlemen and negotiated a deal where I would buy him out of the business," he remembers. "To do that, I had to come up with some quick cash and, although it broke my heart to sell the car, I had no choice to get him out of the business. *Bounty Hunter* will always hold a place in my heart."

After Ed Mueller's ownership, *Bounty Hunter* went to another client of Kevin's, Frank Perulli, and then another, James Korn, and another, Brian Skelton. The waiting list for the car continued to grow even after other black/red 435-hp coupes turned up. Everyone still wanted *Bounty Hunter*.

Recently, the car came up for sale at Mecum, appearing in its factory trim with "Bounty Hunter" decal and mag wheels removed. The car failed to sell after reaching the $350,000 mark; the owner was looking for more than $400,000.

"They took the history away," Kevin feels. "That, to me, made the car really neat. God knows where the wheels are; it took me a while to find the correct wheels."

Don't give up hope just yet of ever seeing *Bounty Hunter* take center stage at a Corvette meet again. Kevin still dreams of showing it again, either for himself or a client, in its historic *Bounty Hunter* trim. In fact, his real goal is slightly loftier: "My goal is to show three black cars together with different color interiors. Have a red interior with a red hood stripe and redline tires; then have a black car with blue interior, blue hood stripe, and bluelines on it; and finally have a black car with white interior, white hood stripe, and whitewalls on it. So you have the three cars: red, white, and blue. Tuxedo Black and white are the only two colors that can have any color interior. The other two are out there, but there aren't many. There's a black/blue convertible that just went for $825,000.

"One day I'll put that collection together. It can be done."

CHAPTER 3

1969 L88 *Rebel* #57

DIXIELAND DELIGHT

The #57 *Rebel* Corvette is one of the most recognizable race cars of all time thanks to its unique Stars & Bars paint scheme. Oh, and the fact that it was the only C3 to score back-to-back wins at Sebring and Daytona in the same year while achieving the highest finish for Corvette, fourth overall, at Sebring.

The Rebel was originally ordered from Ferman Chevrolet in Tampa, Florida, as a 1969 Daytona Yellow convertible. Corvette racer Or Costanzo ordered the car with a complete L88 racing package, one of four lightweights built under the supervision of Zora Arkus-Duntov. Unlike the other three, this one was equipped with a dual disc clutch, making it the only known example. These particular L88s were also built with aluminum open-chamber heads six months before that option became available to L88 buyers and racers. Other special racing equipment included an M22 heavy-duty 4-speed, J56 heavy-duty disc brakes (with J50 power brake option), and F41 heavy-duty suspension. A black vinyl interior came with the car, although it didn't remain in it for very long, and a bolt-on auxiliary hardtop was tacked on.

Like most racers, much of the car's factory options included equipment that was purposefully left off as part of the lightweight package. The heater, convertible top, sound-deadening material, and carpeting were all removed before shipping from St. Louis, Missouri, to Florida. The car that became the famous *Rebel* was stripped even further upon delivery, fitted with fender flares to cover wider wheels and tires, and received a header and sidepipe system to achieve maximum horsepower. This special race equipment was placed into the car at GM Engineering to be installed by the buyer. Engineers called it the "trunk option." They also put an oil cooler in a box inside the car. Other special racing cars besides the lightweight Corvettes were given the "trunk option" as well.

Racing History

The car was driven by Costanzo and Dave Heinz in the 1969 Sebring 12-hour against the best American and European teams of the day. In its first Sebring appearance, Costanzo and Heinz achieved a surprising second-place qualifying run and a third-place finish

The 1969* Rebel *#57 beautifully brought back to its Sebring livery by Corvette Repair. The high-mount mirror, auxiliary driving lights, aluminum diffuser, and covered headlights meant that this car was destined for greatness on the racetrack.

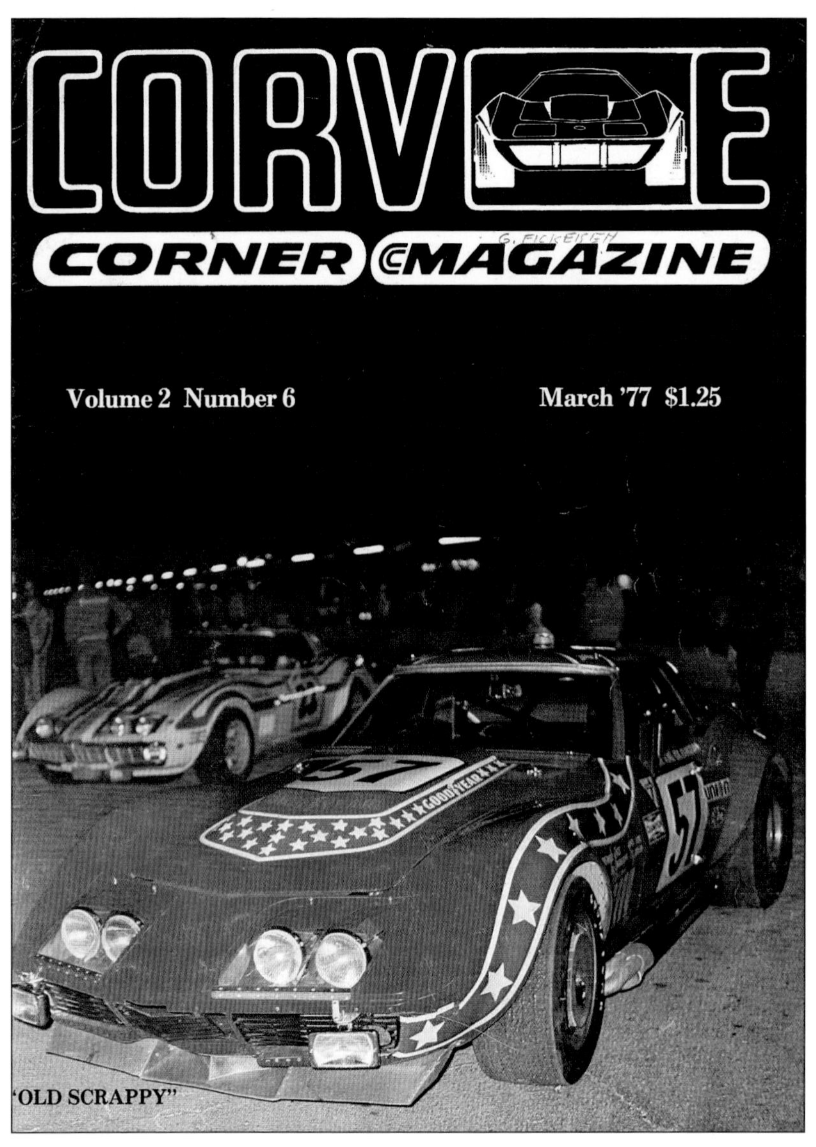

Corvette magazines played a key role in helping Kevin find and confirm the Rebel *Corvette. The first time he saw the car was on the cover of the March 1977 issue of* Corvette Corner, *which he purchased at a swap meet.*

Corvette News *next helped him to identify the car with the June/ July 1972 issue that clearly shows the Le Mans sticker on the bottom left of the rear window.*

in the GT class, major accomplishments for a team with no major sponsorship or professional drivers. The team saw continued success throughout that year's Sports Car Club of America (SCCA) season, where it competed against purebred race cars instead of factory-built tourers. In 1970, a mechanical failure forced a dropout at Sebring after a fifth-place GT class finish at its first Daytona 24-hour.

It wasn't until 1971, however, that the one-off L88 actually became *The Rebel*. The car was completely rebuilt with its now-famous #57 Stars & Bars treatment, which was done as a response to Greenwood Racing's American flag paint scheme. All Dave Heinz's previous race cars carried the number 57 (I'll let you guess why) and Bob Johnson replaced Or Costanzo as co-driver. Although it won four of the five International Motor Sports Association (IMSA) events in 1971, and took the first-ever GTO championship, *the Rebel* still only finished second in the GT class at both Daytona and Sebring, although it had led Daytona for a while until an electrical fire forced a pit road repair. After the 1971 season, Dana and Toye English (son and father) purchased the car, and the team continued to make improvements in terms of lightening and performance.

The year 1972 brought *the Rebel* Corvette to the forefront of the racing world, even with its drivers and lack of a major sponsor. *The Rebel* was driven to first place in the GT class and eighth overall at the 1972 24 Hours of Daytona. Then, just a few weeks later, *the Rebel* took the GT class checkered flag again at Sebring and an astounding fourth-place overall finish. The only cars to finish ahead of the three-year-old Corvette at Sebring were prototype Ferraris. Not only did the 1972 season earn *the Rebel* the title of the only C3 Corvette with back-to-back Sebring and Daytona wins, it still holds the record for the highest finishing factory-built Corvette ever at the 12 Hours of Sebring. It had held the record for highest-placing Corvette at Daytona for 29 years until the C5-R factory team took first-place overall in 2001. It also holds the record of the most-raced Corvette at Sebring, with five total runs (it ran again in 1973).

The Rebel Corvette also served as the test bed for Goodyear's radial tire development program. Goodyear approached *the Rebel* team with a deal right before Daytona. They said, "If you crash the car in the race, you don't know us, but if you win, we'll put you on the cover of the *Wall Street Journal*." Of course, they won, and Goodyear came out with a full-page advertisement in the *Wall Street Journal* championing its new radial tires.

Part of *the Rebel*'s lore lies in its chief competitors, the stars-and-stripes BFG Greenwood Corvettes. "When those two cars would race together," Kevin Mackay says, "they'd say the Civil War had started again because you've got the American flag car and the Confederate flag car. But *the Rebel* car won more races not because it was the most powerful, fastest car on the track, but because it was the most durable car. You can have the fastest car on the track, but if you blow engines and rear ends and transmissions, you're not going to win races. Even though it wasn't as fast, it was so much more durable than the BFG Greenwood cars."

The #49 happened to be the promotional car for BFGoodrich's radial tire program in addition to #48 and #50. So we now know who won that top-secret matchup as well.

Lost and Found

The Rebel Corvette continued to race for some time with various owners and different paint schemes and modifications until eventually, like many glorious race cars, it was forgotten and lost to time. Then, as though fate stepped in, Kevin Mackay was at a swap meet in Mahwah, New Jersey, in the summer of 1990, looking through some old magazines for sale. The vendor had crates upon crates of Corvette magazines piled up and was selling them for $1 each. One such publication was *Corvette Corner,* which featured the Confederate flag race car on the cover. Kevin forked over a dollar to read the whole article once he got home. The article went in-depth about *the Rebel* car being one of four special lightweight L88s, this particular one having been ordered by Or Costanzo as a yellow car. Following his successes with the car, he sold it to Dana and Toye English.

After finishing the article, Kevin picked up the phone and dialed information in search of Or Costanzo in Tampa, Florida. Within 30 seconds he had the phone number for the original owner and driver and wasted no time in dialing it. Or Costanzo was pleasant over the phone, a true Corvette enthusiast; however, Kevin was hardly the first Corvette hunter who had reached out to him.

"That's a very famous car, Kevin," Or told him. "Nobody knows where the car is. I get calls all the time from people asking where it is."

In addition to confirming the sale to his good friends Dana and Toye English, Costanzo had the good heart to relay the car's VIN over the phone. He also mentioned that he still had the original documentation and some parts for the car if anyone were to ever find it.

Kevin's next move was to talk with Dana English. The conversation took an interesting turn when Dana revealed that although he couldn't remember who he sold the car to, he knew that he was a New Yorker who was in the dry-cleaning business but then became an attorney. Kevin's proximity to New York allowed him and his hired sleuth, David Reisner, to come up with a name that fit the somewhat strange set of information: Alex Davidson.

Davidson was perplexed as to how he was tracked down given the number of years that had passed. Kevin wasted no time in getting a confirmation that he did indeed buy a Corvette race car in Tampa, Florida, from Toye English. However, he had sold it many years before and couldn't remember anything about the buyer.

Kevin let him sit for a month before calling back and asking if he could recall anything else. Davidson said that the gentleman was from either North or South Carolina, but he couldn't remember anything else. Kevin gave him another month before calling again; this time Davidson became aggravated.

"Listen, Kevin," he said, "all I can tell you is that it was a doctor named Charlie. I don't remember his last name, and now you're being a pest."

"So now I got either North Carolina or South Carolina and Dr. Charles something," Kevin says. But it was something, and Kevin had a source that had proved to be helpful in finding the John Paul car with little and poor information. He called Harry Hanley, who had records of every car and driver who ever competed in SCCA racing and gave him what little information he had. Just a few weeks later, Hanley called Kevin with a hit. A Dr. Charles West from Greenwood, South Carolina, had raced a 1969 Corvette.

"Don't forget, this is September 1991," Kevin says, "so we're only going back about 15 years to the 1970s. There's a chance this guy's still alive and there's a chance he's still practicing."

Kevin called information looking for Dr. Charles West, who he discovered was a dentist and was still practicing. He called the office number asking for Dr. Charles West to which the response on the other end came back, "Oh, would you like to make an appointment?"

"No," Kevin said. "Just tell him I want to talk about Corvettes."

The receptionist knew that Dr. West was a big car guy and immediately retrieved him.

"Hello, sir, my name's Kevin Mackay and I understand you used to race Corvettes?"

"Yeah," replied Dr. West. "I haven't done it in a while, but yeah."

"Do you have a '69 Corvette?"

Once again, Kevin was cautiously asked how he had gotten his information. He said he got his name from Alex Davidson.

"Oh yeah, I bought the car from Alex. I still have the car, but I kinda junked it."

"What do you mean you kinda junked it?" Kevin asked, perplexed.

It turns out that Dr. West also owned a local junkyard and had dropped the car there in the 1970s. Kevin asked to see it and was invited down, although simultaneously informed that the car wasn't for sale. He was given the doctor's home number to set up a meeting time.

Kevin planned to be in Atlanta, Georgia, a couple of weeks later so he called Dr. West and gave him the only date that he could feasibly drive up to South Carolina and see the car. The date didn't work, as Dr. and Mrs. West had a wedding that day. Kevin said that he would be driving three hours to see the car and didn't know when he'd be

With a paint scheme like this, it's no wonder that the team put a special license plate on the car. The plate was the final piece of the puzzle that Kevin spent years searching for after the car was completed. Also note the little round sticker in the lower left-hand corner of the rear window. That's the Le Mans team sticker that helped Kevin identify the car in that South Carolina junkyard in the middle of the night.

able to make it back.

"Kevin, if you're coming out here from New York, and you can meet me at the wedding place at midnight, I'll make an effort to show you the car."

As soon as he could leave the show he was attending, Kevin got in his rental car and drove the three hours to Greenwood, South Carolina, timed to arrive at the wedding reception hall at midnight. Dr. West came out in a tux and his wife was wearing an evening gown. He commented that it was no problem at all and he was happy to show Kevin the car.

At the junkyard, Dr. West put a set of overalls over his tuxedo at his wife's request, grabbed a flashlight, unlocked the fence gate, and took Kevin on foot into the junkyard. It was one in the morning. West pointed to a big blue boat tarp and said, "There it is."

Kevin walked up and began rolling back the tarp, the faded, deteriorated cover shattering in his hands. He saw Alex Davidson's name on the door immediately. The VIN matched the one that Or Costanzo had given him. Yellow paint peeked out from behind the white that it had been painted since its *Rebel* days. But it wasn't until he looked at the little sticker on the back window that Kevin began "shaking like a leaf." The sticker was the one only given to race teams that competed in the 1972 Le Mans.

This little sticker helped Kevin immediately nail the identification of* the Rebel *Corvette. Its teammate, the #4 Corvette raced by NART, competed at Le Mans and both cars were given these commemorative stickers.

"I have a picture of the car on the cover of *Corvette News* and it's got the sticker," Kevin says. "Bingo! Son of a gun!"

Unfortunately, *the Rebel* Corvette was such a highly modified race car that it didn't qualify for entry into the GT class. Team owner Toye English put together another Corvette to race in France, known as the #4 Rebel Le Mans car. Because both cars were owned by Toye English, he received a commemorative 1972 Le Mans sticker to put on each car. Even though #57 didn't go to Le Mans, it still got a sticker. After the two cars raced together back in the States, the Le Mans car was later sold to Alex Davidson as well, and was later discovered by Jack Boxstrom and restored by Corvette Repair.

Kevin turned to Dr. West and said, "Doc, I've gotta buy this car."

But the good doctor wasn't interested in selling. After Kevin asked repeatedly Dr. West asked, "What do you want to do with this car, Kevin?"

Kevin told Dr. West how he wanted to restore it back to its heyday. Dr. West knew the car was special but didn't otherwise know a whole lot about it. What he did know was that he liked the idea of seeing the car restored, and what he really wanted was to once again own a Porsche that he used to race and had been thinking about buying back. The Porsche would cost him $7,000.

He offered Kevin a deal. "If you give me enough money to buy my old race Porsche back, I'll give you this car. It'll cost you seven grand."

"Deal." Kevin handed him $1,000 in cash as a deposit and said he'd be back in the next couple of days with the rest of the money and to pick up the car.

"He said, 'You really want this car?'" Kevin remembers.

"I said, 'Yeah, I know it's a wreck, but it's real and I'd love to have it.' I remember that I was so numb I couldn't believe I found this damn thing. So I went back to the show the next day and then got home quickly."

Once back at Corvette Repair on Long Island, Kevin hired his friend Billy, who operated a flatbed truck, to bring back the remains of *the Rebel* race car.

"I'll tell ya, that was one of the happiest days of my life, finding that car, because that car is probably the most significant C3 on the planet. They put a 1973 nose on it, but the car was intact. Was it rough? Absolutely, but it was real."

Kevin's trophy, as it sits securely in the Corvette Repair lot after being secured. The high-mount mirror is long gone and the front end was replaced with a later-model bumper. The headlights were also covered up, meaning that this car was used exclusively for short, daytime races.

Restoration Begins

Once the junkyard find arrived safely back at Corvette Repair, Kevin grabbed his dossier and began comparing the notes, photographs, and documents that he had amassed on the car to what was actually sitting in front of him. He then began the arduous process of compiling the complete history of the car, starting once again at the beginning with Or Costanzo. Costanzo this time suggested that Kevin contact Walt Thurn, the original public relations manager and photographer for *the Rebel* team.

Kevin called him and told him that he had found and currently had in his possession *the Rebel* Corvette. Thurn more or less laughed him off. "Yeah, you and everybody else thinks they have that car," Thurn arrogantly stated over the phone. "Mr. Mackay, if you've got that car I'll know you have it because there are some very unique things on that car that only I know about and I've got the photographs to prove it."

Although confident that he had the car, Kevin relished the opportunity to prove it and leave no doubt. He welcomed the expert critical evaluation that Thurn could provide. He suggested that he would shoot a 36-frame roll of film (before the time of digital photography)

When Kevin sent a roll of film to original team photographer Walt Thurn, it was this image that sealed the deal. Thurn immediately recognized the steering wheel and switch console as having been removed from Dave Heinz's boat. In addition, all the gauges were original to the #57 car.

of the car and its details and overnight it to Thurn.

"You son of a gun!" came Walt Thurn's voice over the phone just a day later. He was out of breath. "You got the car! I can't believe you got the car! I developed your 36 prints, Mr. Mackay, and let me tell you, that car is so significant and I can't believe it survived.

"The interior of that car is exactly the way it raced at Sebring. That steering wheel came out of Dave Heinz's boat. That control panel is from Dave Heinz's boat. The shifter and all the gauges are there and the original roll bar. The car is unbelievable. That's the car! I can help you because I have all the photographs of the car in its period."

With a bevy of original photos by Walt Thurn, as well as his enthusiastic approval that this was indeed the real #57 Rebel Corvette, the Corvette Repair team got down to the restoration. All the original wiring was still in place, although the engine and transmission had long since been removed. The steering wheel and control panel from Dave Heinz's boat were refurbished, with every toggle switch still being in serviceable condition.

The final piece of the restoration proved to be one of the most difficult to find, but the car would remain just shy of ultimate perfection until it was attained. When the car raced at Sebring in 1972, the year it made the cover of *Corvette News*, it ran with a novelty plate that featured an image of a Confederate soldier holding a Rebel flag and stated, "Save Yo' Confederate Money Boys—The South Gonna Rise Again!"

Before the Internet and online auction and sales websites, the only way to find something that specific was to stumble upon it at a swap meet. Kevin took the time to poke through license plates at every swap meet he went to and always asked the vendors about this specific one. He finally found it at the Belmont racetrack swap meet and nearly fainted. The restoration of arguably the greatest C3 Corvette was complete.

The Most Valuable

The restored *Rebel* in its 1972 Sebring livery was finished just in time to debut at the 1994 Malcolm Konner Chevrolet Show, the same one where Kevin debuted his first restoration a decade prior. Zora Arkus-Duntov, father of the Corvette, made an appearance to sit in and sign the car.

It was next invited to appear in the newly opened National Corvette Museum among the best 50 Corvettes in existence. "100,000 people were at the museum for the opening and my car was there," Kevin says. "I was like a proud father. That's why I did that car before the John Paul car. I wanted to do the most significant cars first, not even knowing that I would find this car!

"I found it in September 1991 and I found the Sunray DX #3 racer in August 1991. Back to back. Within eight weeks I had two of the most significant cars. I had the best '68 on the planet and the best '69 on the planet just by dumb luck."

The Rebel sat at the museum entertaining, educating, and inspiring Corvette enthusiasts for a year and a half before returning to Kevin's garage to join the Sunray DX #3 Corvette and the VV Cooke Corvette. After years of continuing to show the car, and displaying at Bloomington Gold Special Collection, *the Rebel* received an NCRS American Heritage Award in 2000. Numerous production models, posters, and other promotional material were sold commemorating *the Rebel* Corvette. It would have been tough to be a Corvette enthusiast in the 1990s without hearing about or seeing *the Rebel* and its magnificent story and restoration.

Selling a high-profile race car such as* the Rebel *Corvette comes with its fair share of publicity. Here, Kevin is being interviewed for a television show. He dressed up for the occasion and matches the car perfectly!

In 2014, what had become known as the most iconic L88 Corvette to ever race hit the auction block at Barrett-Jackson Scottsdale. Even with a reserve, *the Rebel* hammered at a record $2.86 million, making it the most valuable C3 Corvette race car ever sold at auction.

Zora Arkus-Duntov sitting in the* Rebel *Corvette that was part of the elite lightweight L88 program. He was personally involved with each one, with* the Rebel *being the most successful on the racetrack. (Photo Courtesy Bill Erdman)

CHAPTER 4

1969 John Paul Lightweight L88

CRIMINALLY FAST

In 1955, after Mercedes's famous accident at Le Mans that led to the deaths of 83 spectators, the major automakers formed a gentlemen's agreement that they would no longer participate in racing. It wasn't that they suddenly realized the danger and wanted to shy away, they feared congressional action that would start with the removal of factory racing. So the major OEMs decided that they would have no *official* involvement going forward. Independent shops popped up staffed by former employees almost immediately and, with silent factory support, turned out high-level competition racers to bear the moniker's flag.

This underground support continued with great success until General Motors ordered all its brands to cease racing operations, public and clandestine. The problem this time was that General Motors was selling too many cars; it had cornered approximately 53 percent of the U.S. market. As it neared 60 percent, government trust busters would be forced to break up the firm under monopoly laws.

As with the previous pullback from racing, GM execs were pulled back in just a few years later when development of the high-performance Mark IV race engine began in 1965 and first saw track use in 1966. Only 13 Corvettes were Heavy-Duty Mark IV equipped in 1966, each one ordered through Zora Arkus-Duntov.

By 1969, factory L88 cars had become a popular starting point for both professional and amateur sportsmen, with 116 being produced that year. They were available through Chevrolet dealerships and, in theory, anyone with the money and desire to drive a bare-bones automobile that required high-octane fuel could buy and drive one. Arkus-Duntov wanted to build more than just a "showroom" amateur race car and decided to build four special lightweight L88s to be given to certain race teams that could bring high-value wins to the Corvette brand.

The four lightweight Corvettes were given special treatment right from the assembly line. Usually, every car was given a water test, which showed any leaks in the body that would have to be fixed before shipping. The lightweight cars were noted "No Water Test" on their build sheets because they were meant for racing only. The cars had no carpets or any other "luxury" features of the other 112 L88s built that year.

Each lightweight was a different color. The white one went to Owens/Corning, the yellow went to *the Rebel* team, the blue one went to Herb Caplan in California (who ended up being the Northwest Champion in 1970), and the burgundy one went to 1964 BP National Champion Frank Dominianni.

John Paul Sr. (right) leans up against his Corvette. His son, successful racer John Paul Jr., has his back to the camera. The father-son duo would go on to race together in the coming years. (Photo Courtesy Kevin Mackay Collection)

Yard Sale

Frank Dominianni's shop, High Speed & Power, had been in business in Valley Stream, New York, since 1946. He became and remained friends with many of the GM engineers and managers in those early days, including Zora Arkus-Duntov. In addition to being the B Production national champion in 1964, he led many race teams to many victories until his death in 2012. His shop also happened to be four blocks away from Corvette Repair.

In 1987, Frank walked into Corvette Repair and said, "You know, Kevin, I've been there a long time, I'm not getting any younger. I've got a lot of stuff and since I know you're into Corvettes, maybe you'd be interested in buying some things from me."

Kevin followed him back to his shop to look around and possibly grab anything Corvette related. He started by putting together piles of parts such as brake shoes, calipers, transmission parts, and cylinder heads; anything that would have been used on a Corvette. He figured that by making a nice pile, he'd be able to get a better deal on everything. Frank just wanted to get rid of the mass collection of parts that he'd been building for 41 years.

"It's like a shrine in there," Kevin says. "He's got stuff everywhere,

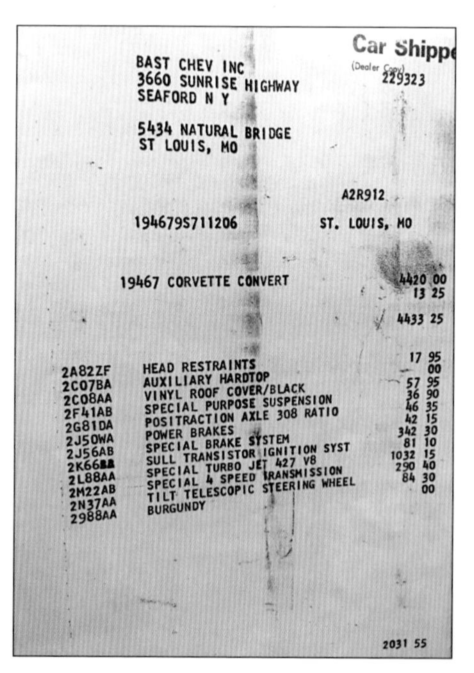

Car Shipp
(Dealer Copy)
229323

BAST CHEV INC
3660 SUNRISE HIGHWAY
SEAFORD N Y

5434 NATURAL BRIDGE
ST LOUIS, MO

A2R912

194679S711206
ST. LOUIS, MO

19467 CORVETTE CONVERT
4420 00
13 25
4433 25

2A82ZF
2C07BA
2C08AA
2F41AB
2G81DA
2J50WA
2J56AB
2K66BB
2L88AA
2M22AB
2N37AA
2988AA

HEAD RESTRAINTS
AUXILIARY HARDTOP
VINYL ROOF COVER/BLACK
SPECIAL PURPOSE SUSPENSION
POSITRACTION AXLE 308 RATIO
POWER BRAKES
SPECIAL BRAKE SYSTEM
SULL TRANSISTOR IGNITION SYST
SPECIAL TURBO JET 427 V8
SPECIAL 4 SPEED TRANSMISSION
TILT TELESCOPIC STEERING WHEEL
BURGUNDY

17 95
00
57 95
36 90
46 35
42 15
342 30
81 10
1032 15
290 40
84 30
00

2031 55

Once Frank Dominianni spoke with Arkus-Duntov about his special racing Corvette, he ordered the car through Bast Chevrolet in Seaford, New York. This shipping report shows every special option that was fitted to the car along with its cost and RPO number. The option that caught Kevin's eye was fourth from the bottom: 2L88AA SPECIAL TURBO JET 427 V-8 for $1,032.15. Other notable options to Corvette enthusiasts are the M22 transmission, J56 brakes, and F41 suspension. The whole car cost Robert Essex $6,464.80.

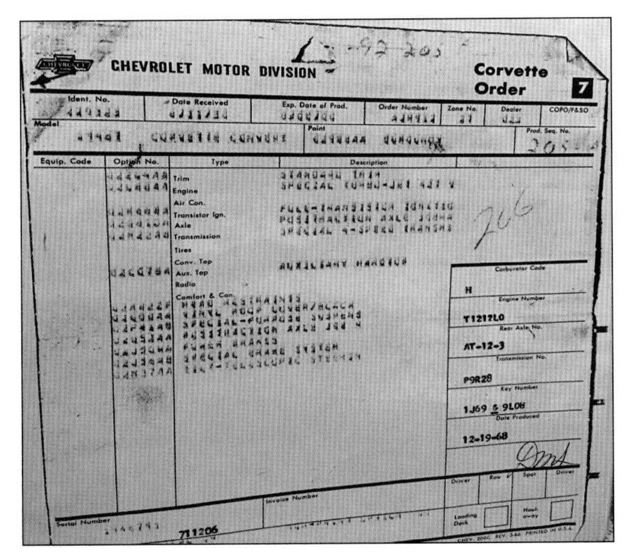
CHEVROLET MOTOR DIVISION

Corvette Order 7

Ident. No. | Date Received | Exp. Date of Prod. | Order Number | Zone No. | Dealer | COPO/F&SO

Model | Paint | Prod. Seq. No.

Equip. Code | Option No. | Type | Description

Trim
Engine
Air Con.
Transistor Ign.
Axle
Transmission
Tires
Conv. Top
Aux. Top
Radio
Comfort & Con.

Carburetor Code: H
Engine Number: T1217LO
Rear Axle No.: AT-12-3
Transmission No.: P9R28
Key Number: 1J69 5 9L08
Date Produced: 12-19-68

Driver | Row | Spot | Driver
Invoice Number
Loading Dock | Haul-away
Serial Number
711206

The amount of documentation that Frank Dominianni had kept over the years was astounding and made finding the original car that much more special. This document is called "Copy Number Seven," which is a duplicate of the original gas tank sticker that holds every bit of information about a car. All the serial numbers are noted along with the list of options and ordering information. Copy Number Seven is vital to identifying the car's original components when the gas tank and sticker are gone.

you name it, since 1946! You can imagine what it looks like in there. You couldn't even walk in the place there was so much stuff in there."

With four decades of significant racing history in one spot, Kevin asked Frank if he could "snoop around a little bit." Frank allowed it, so Kevin went back into his office to find plaques, trophies, awards, and photographs on the walls of Corvettes that Frank had been involved with. "That was back when I was young and wild," Frank told Kevin. "I was pretty good at it. I won the National Championship in 1964, beat out Don Yenko in the points."

Kevin asked if he could look through his cabinets for anything of interest. Frank replied, "Go ahead. I can't take this stuff with me."

As he went through the file cabinets, Kevin spied a folder named "Sebring Corvettes." He opened it to find a car shipper report, which is a carbon copy of a car's window sticker. The car it was attached to was ordered through Bast Chevrolet in Seaford, New York, and included the car's serial number and list of options.

"So I go down the list and there it is. Bingo!" Kevin says. "L88 Special Turbo-Jet 427. Son of a gun! That's one of 116 cars produced. Even back then those cars were bringing close to $100,000."

He continued going through the paperwork, finding it remarkably complete. Frank had "Copy Number Seven," which is a copy of the gas tank sticker that's on the car. He had key numbers, engine numbers, the complete auto transit report, everything. The car was originally ordered from Bast Chevrolet, but it was shipped to Gene Jantzen Chevrolet, which is right across the street from the St. Louis plant. Because General Motors frowned upon race teams picking up cars at the plant, they used Gene Jantzen Chevrolet as a cover for what would have otherwise been factory pickups.

"Oh yeah, I went there," Frank recalled after Kevin asked him about what he had discovered. "This guy named Bob Essex, very wealthy guy in New York City, big into real estate, hired me to build him a race car. I told him the best way to build a race car is to get one of these L88s. 'Let's fly out to Detroit and meet with the engineers there and maybe we can get a special car built.'"

Frank and Bob flew to Detroit to meet privately with Arkus-Duntov and a few other engineers, who told them about the four special lightweight L88s. Only certain teams would be given the cars and because Frank had been a national champion, Arkus-Duntov would give one to him as long as he promised to build it and race it. Frank told them how Bob wanted to get into racing and was financing the operation, but reiterated that he was 100 percent in charge.

Only one question remained: "What color do you want?"

Frank wanted a red car, but Bob told him that he was colorblind and red appeared to him as maroon. So they decided on a burgundy car.

On the car's build sheet that Kevin held in his hand appeared the words, "No Water Test." Kevin knew that the car was something special and was "shaking like a leaf" as he put it with his pile of parts.

Not only was it a documented L88, there were secret letters from General Motors in the folder about how to run the oil lines and set up the car, telegrams about ordering special brake pads and Sylvania lighting for racing. There was a letter from Ed Lowther, a driver who was involved with Don Yenko. There was documentation from the car having raced at Sebring. Frank Dominianni had saved everything.

After agreeing on prices for the parts in his pile, Kevin turned to Frank and asked how much the folder and its contents would cost. Frank wanted $50, a more than fair price, Kevin thought. He paid him and left, taking the folder with him, and planning to return later to pick up the parts.

"I can't believe it," Kevin remembers thinking when he got back to his shop and sorted through the Sebring Corvette's folder. "I have all this paperwork. I have to go find this car; it's got to be worth a fortune!

"This car started my hunt for rare cars. I could never afford an L88 at the time. I was a young guy, just turned 30 years old, and this would be a dream come true if I could find an L88 car that went to Sebring, Daytona, and was one of four lightweights."

How Do You Spell "Essex"?

After he secured all the paperwork and did as much background research as he could, Kevin returned to Frank Dominianni to ask him more about his partnership with Bob Essex and how he could find him to begin tracing the car. "Yes, Kevin, the guy is just a rich ***hole. I don't like the guy; we had a big fallout."

"Frankie's a bit of a hothead also," according to Kevin. "But this guy Bob Essex was also a hothead, so that's probably where those guys clashed. I asked where Bob Essex lived."

"I don't know, Kevin, the guy's some rich guy, I don't know much about him. I was with him for not even a year. We raced at Daytona, raced at Sebring, then we had a big fallout. We were supposed to go to The Glen, but he did his own thing and I cut ties with him. That's all I can tell you."

"How do you spell Essex?" Kevin asked.

"I don't know, E-S-S-E-X?"

Kevin started by going through all the phone books in the area looking for Robert Essex. He went to the library for more phone books once his local ones turned into dead ends. He repeated "E-S-S-E-X" every time he ran his finger down the page. Nothing.

Then an idea popped into his head. "To race at Sebring or Daytona you gotta have a special racing license through the SCCA. I contacted the SCCA, and the guy who ran the archives department was a guy named Harry Hanley. I told him I was looking for a guy named Robert Essex, E-S-S-E-X; he raced a 1969 Corvette."

A week later Harry Hanley called him back, asking if he was sure he had the right spelling. Kevin said that he wasn't sure; he's a very bad speller. Hanley told him he had found a Robert Esseks, spelled E-S-S-E-K-S, and gave him an old address.

"E-S-S-E-K-S!" Kevin shouted when he got off the phone. "A *K* instead of an *X*, goddammit!"

Kevin found out that Esseks had moved nine times since then.

As he went through telephone books all over again, he still couldn't find anything. Finally, he discovered a woman in Queens, New York, named Patricia Esseks. He called her and said he was looking for Robert Esseks.

"What do you want with that jerk?" came the woman's voice on the other end.

Although he assumed he had the right guy, Kevin asked if he used to race Corvettes.

"Oh yeah," she replied. "He raced Corvettes and Cobras. Look, we had a bad marriage, and I don't like the guy. He's alive somewhere in Connecticut. Don't call here ever again. I don't want to hear that name ever again. Now I'm all upset."

She hung up the phone, but at least Kevin learned that Bob Esseks was alive and in Connecticut. After months of searching, he turned up nothing, and asked a law enforcement customer of his to help him run the name Robert Esseks. E-S-S-E-K-S.

Esseks, as it turned out, was living on a boat, had a Connecticut driver's license, and a P.O. Box. Kevin wrote him a letter.

"I had to lie and tell him I had the car," Kevin says. "I knew where the car came from, who drove the car, who had the car, and who worked on the car. I was afraid that if I told him I was looking for it, he'd clam right up. I couldn't take that chance with all this documentation. I knew that Corvette better than anybody, and after all the research and collecting I had done on it, I had to find out who had the car. So I told him I had the car already."

It didn't take Esseks long to call Kevin back after receiving his letter. "So you got my old race car, huh?" he said. Kevin points out that he was very nice over the phone, hardly living up to the reputation of those closest to him. He then relayed the same story that Frank had already told Kevin about the trip to Engineering in Detroit, wanting a burgundy car instead of a red one, and how Frank picked it up and drove it back from Gene Jantzen Chevrolet to break in the engine. He said that when they campaigned the car at Daytona a wheel fell off and they were disqualified.

"We went to Sebring and the car crapped out there, too. Me and Frankie parted ways. I sold the car to a guy named John Paul."

"You mean John Paul Sr.?" Kevin asked.

"Yeah, he took over where Frankie left off and we did quite well with the car for a while. Eventually, I sold the car to John. You may have a tough time finding him, though. He got himself in trouble with the law. He was smuggling drugs into the country and selling them, and when they caught him, he shot an FBI agent to escape. They found him somewhere in Switzerland. He's in prison. I don't know where. Good luck, and let me know how the car's coming out."

Selling Drugs to Fund a Racing Addiction

Kevin's next objective was to find John Paul Sr. He called up another friend of his in law enforcement and asked for help in locating him in the prison system. His friend said, "Kevin, isn't that the guy who was a racer and to support his habit he was selling marijuana? He's a bad guy; he shot a witness!"

"I just want to talk Corvettes with the guy," Kevin responded.

The friend called him back later that day. "Listen to me, Kevin. I just want to tell you right now this guy is bad. He made an escape attempt in Florida. He tried to hop over the fence. He made some Tabasco sauce into pepper spray and threw it in a guard's face. There was a stolen truck with keys in the ignition. This is a bad, bad guy. He shot a guy five times and he lived. He's in prison for 25 years."

"I just want to talk to the guy."

"Okay, they moved him from Florida to Leavenworth, Kansas, where he's in maximum security. You're not gonna get ahold of him; you have to write him a letter. Maybe, if he's on good behavior, they'll put him on a payphone and he'll call you. That's the best you can do."

That's exactly what Kevin did. He wrote a letter introducing himself and saying that he was in possession of his old race car. Not long after that, he received a collect call from Leavenworth Penitentiary.

"I had John Paul Sr. on the phone," Kevin says. "I'll tell ya, he was the nicest guy to me. I hear they call him "The Pirate" because he had a very bad temper. Now this guy was a very intelligent guy; he was a Harvard grad. When he was smuggling drugs from South America he was making an average of $300,000 a year, in the 1970s. That's like a million dollars today!"

Racing is expensive. Between the crew, lodging, transportation, and the actual costs associated with the car such as fuel, tires, and parts, it takes a lot of money to compete at a high level. John Paul Sr. believed that the best and fastest way to make the kind of money necessary was to smuggle marijuana. That was until he came up with a faster and higher profit method of making money: grow the marijuana in the United States. He built an underground facility the size

The John Paul Corvette sitting at its storage yard. The station wagon behind it was the team hauler. It's a far cry from the massive state-of-the-art facilities used by race teams today! (Photo Courtesy Kevin Mackay Collection)

of a football field and illegally tapped into a nearby electrical junction box to run his fans and lights. His operation boomed and he had more money than ever to race.

Although he had been caught and sentenced to three years' probation and a $32,000 fine, he continued to grow and sell marijuana, now with the help of his son, John Paul Jr. In 1984, Stephen Carson agreed to testify against him as a federal witness in exchange for immunity from prosecution. Paul Sr. shot him five times after he refused to get into his trunk. After turning himself in and being released on bond, he fled to Switzerland, where he was caught a year later attempting to withdraw money from his secret Swiss bank account. Even with his escape attempt, he was paroled in 1999 after serving only 13 of 25 years.

The John Paul Sr. story gets more interesting when you add the fact that this his second wife disappeared in 1981, and, after his prison release, his girlfriend disappeared on the couple's boat trip around the world. Paul Sr. was never charged in his wife's disappearance; however, he disappeared after his girlfriend's disappearance and hasn't been seen since 2001. He's still wanted for questioning, although he currently faces no charges.

"Anyway, I got this guy on the phone who's probably a murderer (this is before he got out again)," Kevin gets back on track. "He has a photographic memory. He sent me a letter back with all the details about what he did to the car, and he says he sold the car to a guy named Rodney Harris."

To the Glen

Kevin easily contacted Rodney Harris, who remembered the car and confirmed that he bought it from John Paul. He had wrecked it and rebuilt it during the time that he owned it. He then sold it to someone from New York, near Watkins Glen racetrack, but he couldn't remember his name. It was early 1988 at this point, and Harris sold the car in 1974 or 1975. He did remember that the new owner crashed it at The Glen sometime in the 1970s.

Armed with that information, Kevin began pouring though race results. Then he thought it would be easier just to call up the racetrack and see if there was a historian available to speak with. There was, and Kevin called Bill Green.

"I get ahold of Mr. Green and I said, 'Mr. Green, I have this car and I'm trying to find some history,'" Kevin says. "'It raced at the Watkins Glen six-hour race in 1974 and I know the car crashed. I just want to get some history of the car. Can you tell me who crashed that car in that particular race?'"

Four days went by before Kevin received a phone call from Green. Apparently, two Corvettes had crashed in that race, each sporting two drivers. He relayed the names of all four drivers to Kevin, who dialed Rodney Harris back to see if any of the names would jog his memory.

"Kevin, if you give me the name, I would remember it instantly," he said. "It's at the tip of my tongue and it's been bugging me."

Kevin tells him the first two names. No recollection. Harris's wife was with him when he sold it, and was there on the phone with him to help recall the man's name. Neither name sounded correct to her, either.

Kevin gives the third name: "Tom Rynone."

"That's the guy!" came Harris's voice on the other end of the line. "Honey, Tom Rynone? Yup, that's the guy, Kevin."

Bill Green had been working at Watkins Glen his whole life, and is still there today. He knew Tom Rynone personally, as he was a local resident who owned a trucking firm. He offered to call Rynone and let him know that Kevin had his old race car.

"I got some horrible news for you, Kevin," Green said two days later when he called back. "The car you have is not the car you think it is. He's still got the car."

"That's horrible news!" Kevin cried back into the phone, his excitement veiled in sarcastic misery. "Horrible news! Would you mind if I talk to the guy?"

Tom Rynone picked up the phone when Kevin called and said, "Kevin, I don't know what car you have, but you don't have that car. I crashed it at The Glen in 1974 and, honestly, it must be a different car because I have the car behind my trucking place. It's buried in the dirt. It's been sitting there since the 1970s; it's like a planter."

"I'd love to take a look at it. I've been learning about this car for 11 months. I know so much about this car I'd like to see it."

"You can take a look at it, but the car's a wreck."

After stopping at the bank to empty out his account, which consisted of $8,000 at the time, Kevin drove his flatbed truck six hours up to Watkins Glen, New York. Rynone points out the car; it was buried under 6 inches of dirt. In the dead of March 1988, the ground in upstate New York was covered in snow and frozen solid. Kevin asked Rynone for a shovel and a hatchet so that he could unearth the car to see it better.

"I chopped away with the hatchet and the shovel," Kevin recalls. "It was cold up there; like 20 degrees. My friend Billy and I were up there together. So we dig the trench, attach the winch chains, and drag the thing out into the parking lot. I'm looking at it and I say, 'Tom, I'd like to buy this thing.'"

Rynone asked what Kevin's plans were for the heap of dirt and metal.

"I'm going to restore it back to brand new, and one day I'm going to let you drive the car again."

"You're really going to bring that car back from the dead?"

"Yes."

"Well," Tom Rynone said, "you can have it for free. What am I going to do with it? Look at it. If you can put it back together, knock yourself out."

"The car literally cost me $50," Kevin points out, "because I bought the documentation for $50. So I bought an L88 car for 50 bucks."

A few years later, Kevin found *the Rebel* car, then the Sunray DX car. As his business boomed, he prioritized restoring and showing the most important cars first. Although it has an exciting backstory in addition to being one of four lightweight L88s handpicked by Zora Arkus-Duntov, what Kevin calls "the John Paul racer" wasn't as successful as the others were on the racetrack.

To this day, the originally burgundy, lightweight L88 sits in parts, in storage, waiting to be restored. "Eventually I'll put it together again," Kevin says. "And I gotta do it soon because I'm not getting any younger!"

CHAPTER 5

1969 VV Cooke #80

THE WINNINGEST C3 CORVETTE

By 1969, Chevrolet's L88 race program was in full swing. They were quickly becoming known as some of the fastest cars on the track, and they were often driven by the best Corvette drivers of the day. If you wanted to put up a fight on the racetrack and you had the money and connections, the L88 was it.

Racing History

Doug Bergen was an enthusiast who had been involved in racing for several years before reaching out to Chevrolet about ordering an L88 in 1969. The original car was ordered with black paint and a tan interior, an usual combination for any '69, much less a race car.

Because Bergen purchased the car too late in the 1969 season to compete, it made its debut at the 1970 Daytona 24 Hour. Outfitted with heavy-duty springs and Koni shocks, at the advice of Gib Hufstader, plus fender flares, roll cage, and 42-gallon fuel cell, it debuted as #8. It was driven by "Marietta" Bob Johnson, another driver also named Bob Johnson (nicknamed the Band-Aid drivers since Band-Aid was produced by Johnson & Johnson), and Jim Greendyke. Unfortunately, it dropped out of the race after 457 laps and received a DNF.

A couple of months later, the team brought the car, now labeled #3, to the 12 Hours of Sebring, where it received its first taste of success. Although it finished 2nd in the GT class, it managed an 11th-place overall finish out of 68 starters. At this time, VV Cooke, a Chevrolet dealer in Louisville, Kentucky, began to take an interest in Bergen's L88 to keep his own team competitive. Cooke approached Bergen about selling the car, but a deal wasn't struck until later that year at Watkins Glen. In fact, Bob Johnson was sitting in the car on the pre-grid when Bergen told him to get out of the car as he didn't own it anymore!

VV Cooke had a team of brothers, Allan and Don Barker, racing for him. Allan ended up behind the wheel of the recently acquired L88. The story takes a twist here, as the Barkers had previously been successful running small-block cars. The L88 engine was pulled and replaced with a small-block prepared by the legendary TRACO shop. The rare L88 Corvette only ended up seeing two races in that form.

Although the VV Cooke Corvette was originally an L88 big-block, it was later converted to a small-block, which was its championship-winning configuration. The flat hood seen from this angle tells part of that story. The grins on Kevin's and Chip Miller's faces give an idea of what driving this unrestored beauty is like.

The interior of the VV Cooke car had also been left alone over the years and still sported its combination of racing and stock equipment. The brown interior is original, and is one of the few reminders that this was originally Doug Bergen's car.

Back at the VV Cooke shop, the car was treated to an updated paint configuration in addition to the smaller powerplant. Allan Barker went on to win back-to-back SCCA B production national championships in 1971 and 1972. VV Cooke then sold the car to Bill Jobe, who raced the car himself to another set of back-to-back national championships in 1973 and 1974. By the time Jobe relinquished ownership of the car, it had officially become the winningest Corvette in SCCA history.

Bill Jobe never changed the original VV Cooke paint scheme. However, once he sold it to David Preston in 1975, Preston simply changed the white lettering to yellow, painted the wheels yellow, and changed the number to 51. By this time, the small-block had begun to outlive its track effectiveness and Preston enjoyed competing in regional and club events before parking it on his trailer outside his house. At that point, the whereabouts and provenance of the winningest Corvette became lost.

The underside of #80's hood shows off the four national titles that the VV Cooke team won from 1969 to 1972. The 1969 and 1970 titles were from the team's 1963 Z06 fuel-injected roadster; the 1971 and 1972 titles were from #80. Bill Jobe left the car's paint scheme completely untouched, not even to add his own titles in 1973 and 1974 to the running list.

The Hunt for the VV Cooke Racer

The VV Cooke racer, relieved of its L88 engine and battered beyond usefulness, had seemingly no way of being found by the time L88 Corvettes had gone from used race cars to highly sought-after collectibles. A young Kevin Mackay had just started his Corvette Repair business and, although he had the knowledge and skillset, he didn't have the money to go after real, numbers-matching L88 cars. Even in the late 1980s they were going for what he calls "stupid money."

While researching L88s one night and thinking about his recently discovered John Paul race car and others he had come across, a thought popped into his head. All of the L88 race cars that he had seen had originally come with factory heavy-duty options. The M22 transmission and heavy-duty brakes and suspension components were desired by race teams because it was cheaper and less time consuming to buy an L88 from the factory than it was to build one out of a showroom 427.

"Most of these race cars probably started life as factory L88s," Kevin mused to himself. "I found that race cars rarely had engines in them and most had lost their pedigree over time. But if I know it's a factory L88 car, I can get that car for a song and a dance!"

Kevin turned back to his collection of *Corvette News* magazines to create a personal database of all the L88 racers or probable L88 racers he could find. Because *Corvette News* was a Chevrolet publication, cars featured on the cover would likely be of extreme importance, meaning L88. The #80 VV Cooke car happened to be such a cover car and, after some research, Kevin decided to hunt it down.

The first step Kevin took was to call private investigator David Reisner to take on much of the leg work while Kevin tended to his budding business. Reisner poured through phone books and made calls during the day when Kevin was unavailable to track down leads.

"I'd say, 'Listen to me, I want this car,'" Kevin explains, "and he would help me hunt down the car. Once he finds something, he lets me know. Sometimes he may find something, but it could be that the car was stolen or destroyed and the car was gone.We found out that a lot of cars that I was going after were stolen, wrecked, chopped up, or sent to the crusher. So I'd pay for his time to find out the whereabouts of the car or what really happened to it."

Eventually, Reisner was able to track the car to David Preston in Albuquerque, New Mexico. That name resonated with Kevin

To make the cover of **Corvette News,** *a car truly needed to achieve greatness. The 1969 #80 VV Cooke car was no exception, and as the winningest Corvette in history, its place was well-deserved. It also gave Kevin a target to pursue.*

immediately, as he had discovered a list of owners in a magazine from the 1970s, a list that ended with David Preston. As usual, getting an unwilling owner to sell his car requires all the patience and strategy of a chess match, and this car was no different. Preston had dreams of rebuilding the car and putting it back on the road, and he had no desire to sell it. Unfortunately, without revealing his research on the car and the potential value it could muster as a restored example, Kevin didn't have many options.

Kevin remained persistent, yet polite, with David Preston, and year after year he'd get the same response, that he was still planning on putting it back on the road. "I didn't want to piss him off, so I'd say, 'Alright David, no problem at all.' I told him that I'll give the car a great home and I'll give it the restoration it really deserves. I never even saw the car!"

Kevin had a friend, Mike Metzger, a retired gym teacher who worked at North Shore High School on Long Island. He had recently retired and, not knowing what to do with his time, decided to coach baseball, a passionate pastime he had always enjoyed. In the summer, Coach Metzger piled the team into his 12-seater van and drove them across the country, stopping at different stadiums for pro games. Not only did he love to drive, he loved Corvettes, and always offered to help Kevin with his hunts while he was on the road. "I've had Mike running around rattlesnakes looking for cars!"

"Hey, Kevin, you got any projects for me this year?" Metzger asked before one such trip.

"Yeah, why don't you go pay this guy David Preston a visit," Kevin responded. "I want you to drive all the way to Albuquerque, New Mexico [a 2,500-mile run]. And would you please convince him to sell me that car?"

It wasn't too long after that Kevin received a phone call from New Mexico. Metzger said that he had met with David Preston and that he was ready to sell the car.

Kevin's response? "You're kidding me!"

Metzger's third-party approach had been the missing ingredient Kevin needed. "I told him all about you," Metzger told Kevin of his conversation with Preston. "I told him you're a great guy, you've been on the car forever, and that you'd pay a fair price for it. So you better make your move quick!"

Metzger made it home three days later, only to get back on a plane with Kevin, to the tune of $400 a ticket, and head back to New Mexico. They knocked on Preston's door, cash in hand.

"I knocked on his door, and I saw someone walking back and forth through the window, so I knew someone was there," Kevin says. "After 15 minutes, he wouldn't answer the door, and I kept ringing the doorbell and knocking on the door.

"Finally, he answered the door and says, 'You must be Kevin. You're probably very upset with me. I've been jerking you around for all these years.'

"Look, you're selling me the car today. I'm a happy camper!"

They entered his house, an obvious bachelor pad with his belongings and numerous car parts all over the place. Kevin set the money on the pool table and invited Preston to count it. He declined. "Count the money," Kevin said. "I'm from New York, count it anyway, I'd feel better about it." The agreed-upon price was $15,000.

"Well, I paid him the money and the car's just sitting in the driveway on a trailer with four flats. It's probably one of the most original race cars I've ever seen in my life. It still had the original trim from when it won its four national championships. It's all chained down with a cover on it. He had transmissions, rear ends, extra wheels, and extra tires. So I said to myself, 'We flew here, now how the hell am I

The VV Cooke Corvette after a quick sprucing-up at Corvette Repair in New York. Notice the nice, new tires that actually hold air? Other than that, the car was left in as-found condition. It still sported its VV Cooke livery and showed some interesting battle scars, but it wasn't destroyed like the other cars. (Photo Courtesy Bill Erdman)

going to get this thing home? I can't drive this freaking thing out of here!'"

They went to the local U-Haul facility to rent a pickup truck with a hitch. After filling up the trailer tires they worked up a plan. "Who the hell do I know in Albuquerque, New Mexico? I know a guy named Ray Battaglini, who was president of the National Corvette Museum. I'll call him. He turned out to be only 5 miles away. I told him, 'I got this old beat-up race car; you think I could leave it with you for a couple of weeks until I can get a trailer to pick it up?'"

He agreed to help Kevin out, offering a spot in his business lot for the car and trailer. Kevin then rented a storage unit to store all the miscellaneous parts that came with the sale. After flying back to New York, Kevin found a flatbed truck to pick up the car, still on the race trailer, and all of the parts.

"When I finally got that car back from Albuquerque, I put air in the tires, checked inside, oiled the cylinders, and turned the engine over manually. We took the carburetor off and rebuilt it, changed the oil and filter, primed the engine, and put in a new battery. Albuquerque

One of the giveaways that this is a purpose-built race car is the quad red taillights. A regular Corvette has a clear reverse light in the center of the inner lights. A lack of bumpers and exhaust tips, in addition to the deep fuel cell where the spare tire would otherwise go, confirm that this car was meant for the track.

is such a dry climate, there was no rust on the car at all."

The Corvette Repair team inspected the fuel cell and found that the foam had deteriorated, so they had to vacuum out all the pieces before putting in fresh racing fuel. Kevin got behind the wheel, stepped on the gas a couple of times, put some fuel in the rebuilt carburetor, and the veteran racer started right up.

"It ran like a champ," Kevin says. The process took less than two days. Afterward, they mounted a set of NOS racing tires on the wheels, and put the #80 back on the sides and Allan Barker's name on the door.

With the car's complete history now known, Kevin took it to the National Corvette Museum and invited Allan Barker and his brother, Don, to reunite with his old race car. Allan brought his wife and grandkids with him to enjoy the experience, and some of the guys from his pit crew showed up as well! Kevin did similar reunions with Doug Bergen and VV Cooke, and he managed to get some incredible exposure for his shop at the same time.

The Legacy

Unlike most of his finds that are often mangled beyond use, the VV Cooke car was mostly complete and sporting a lifetime of battle scars and bruises from duking it out on the racetrack. After some additional research, Kevin learned that it was the only known, documented black convertible L88 with a saddle interior, adding to its rarity. He badly wanted to restore it to its national championship winning state, but received many recommendations about leaving it in as-found condition. Crowds gathered around the survivor at every show it attended, further increasing the car's exposure.

Kevin loved the car, and fulfilled the dream of adding it to his collection, which consisted of the #57 *Rebel* car and the #3 Sunray DX car. *The Rebel* had received a perfect, concours-level restoration while the Sunray had been turned into one of his unique creations by being cut in half, yet still drivable. The completely unrestored VV Cooke car was the perfect addition to Kevin's garage. All three factory L88 racers had been on the cover of *Corvette News* and each had its

Kevin and his friend Chip Miller preparing to take the VV Cooke racer on the streets at Bloomington Gold at the Roar to Zora event in 1999. Not sure those helmets are going to do much, but you might not want to remember crashing a car like that.

own claim to fame in Corvette lore. *The Rebel* was the only C3 to win back-to-back at Daytona and Sebring in the same year, the Sunray DX not only won at Sebring in 1968 but clocked the highest finish ever for a Corvette, and the VV Cooke car was the winningest Corvette in history, having once won 29 races in a row.

After Kevin sold the car, the new owner opted to compete in vintage races with it, along with the other two cars Kevin sold him. He essentially beat them up in racing. He has since sold *the Rebel* and the Sunray DX, both of which Kevin was able to re-restore, but he still owns the VV Cooke car.

"I gotta get my hands on that car and give it a good home." Kevin says. "Eventually we'll get that car again, and now we're going to restore it because he had someone restore it already, but then he raced it. So now I'm going to bring that car to a beauty queen down the pike." Kevin believes the car could easily be worth a couple million dollars in restored condition.

For those looking for a cheaper alternative to buying a multimillion-dollar L88 Corvette race car, the original Dragstar trailer, the one with the flat tires, is still out there. Kevin sold it to an employee, regrettably breaking up the set. "It was definitely Bill Jobe's because it was titled in his name, but I think it was Allan Barker's original trailer," he says. "It was kinda cool to have it, but in New York, there's no room."

The VV Cooke racer was a special car in its racing heyday, but its discovery in such original condition only improved its legacy. Compared to the other race cars that Kevin has found that are oftentimes not even recognizable, the VV Cooke car is as close to original as can be!

CHAPTER 6

The Sunray DX Cars

In 1965, Sunray DX was the world's sixth largest oil company and made the decision to promote its brand through racing. Specifically, public relations supervisor and sports car enthusiast Ralph Morrison Jr. convinced company executives that marketing their product to drivers, race teams, and spectators would have a worthwhile return. Initially, Sunray sponsored two SCCA events in 1965, one in Arkansas and one in Oklahoma. Sunray provided advertising money for the event, trophies, and oil and gas for the race teams.

The first two events were a huge success for the brand and the 1966 sponsorship calendar was expanded, along with the budget. A driver contingency program was started where drivers who placed a Sunray DX decal on their cars, and finished in a high enough position, could get paid for bringing exposure to the brand. Although it's believed that no driver actually got paid, the huge number of red, white, and blue shield decals brought even more exposure to the brand. Under Morrison's leadership, Sunray DX began to directly sponsor cars in 1967.

Ralph Morrison proved to his bosses at Sunray DX that race sponsorship could be successful, and it was time to take the next step: developing a Sunray DX race team. The choice of vehicle to campaign was important for the image of the brand, and the obvious marque to Morrison was Corvette. The obvious man to make it all happen was Don Yenko and his Canonsburg, Pennsylvania–based Yenko Chevrolet. Yenko was familiar with a new high-performance racing engine being produced by the factory, dubbed the L88, and used his connections to order the very first one. The '67 coupe was ordered in Ermine White with a red interior. Dave Morgan went to St. Louis on March 9, 1967, to pick it up and drive it the 600 miles back to Yenko Chevrolet.

With the 1967 Sebring 12-hour race coming up in three weeks, the Yenko crew went to work prepping the car to compete. The car was stripped of most of the carpeting and interior trim, not that much came from the factory on L88s. A 42-gallon fiberglass fuel tank was installed along with a roll cage and American Racing Torq Thrust wheels and Firestone Goldline tires. The rear fenders received larger flares to cover the wide tires; massive air extractors were installed behind the front wheels to aid in brake cooling. The factory chrome bumpers were removed and the car was given a red racing stripe down the center of the roof to match the stinger and blue paint on the sides.

The #3 Sunray DX car was the first one that Kevin was able to find and purchase. Having started life as a 1968 factory L88, it was first restored as a cutaway car, with one half of the body removed to reveal its inner workings. It was later fully restored and sold as part of Kevin's million-dollar collection in 2000.

Mechanically, Sunray DX #8 was fitted with a special set of L88-specific headers and sidepipes produced by Chevrolet Engineering. It's believed that only 5 to 10 sets were produced for the 20 C2 L88s built. Engineering also provided the Yenko crew with a 2.60:1-ratio differential, which was taller than anything even offered in production cars, the maximum being 2.73:1.

The 1967 Sebring race proved to be a success for the young Sunray DX team, as Morgan and Yenko finished 1st in the GT class and 10th overall, despite a brake failure on lap 195, which forced them to retire. After Sebring, Morgan continued to campaign Sunray DX #8 on his own, taking home that year's SCCA Midwest division championship.

The second L88 Corvette to fly the Sunray colors at Le Mans was ordered through Dana Chevrolet by chief engineer and driver Dick Guldstrand. Dana Chevrolet owners Paul Doski and Peyton Cramer ordered a Marina Blue '67 L88 coupe, but this time with a black

Take a look at the interior of the #8 car. It's barely discernable in most pictures, but this car has a red interior, meaning that it's the one that raced at Sebring in 1967 before being lost. Kevin found this car near Corvette Repair on Long Island, in street trim, but wasn't able to buy it at the time. Unlike other racing Corvettes, #8 still uses its flip-up headlights.

interior. Because the L88s were still developmental cars, Chevrolet retained some control over them, and insisted that this one be left in stock trim, except for required safety and visual alterations. The stock chrome bumpers were even left on the car. Dick Guldstrand objected, wanting to beef up the engine and various aspects of the car for the beating he knew Le Mans would throw at it.

Even without Guldstrand's requested improvements, the #9 Corvette managed to set a record 171 mph on the famed Mulsanne straight. After 167 laps, and in its 13th hour, the wrist pins failed while the car was leading the GT class, forcing it out of the race. For those wondering, yes, that was part of Guldstrand's initial race prep concept that he wasn't allowed to do.

The Sunray DX Corvette race team had proven its might in the international racing arena, unlike Sunray's other effort involving McLaren Chevrolet and its Lola T-70. With Can-Am racing out of the picture, the Corvette side of things was given a big boost in funding, allowing two 1968 Corvettes from Yenko Chevrolet to compete alongside the '67 car #31 (now #8), all of which were outfitted in traditional DX red, white, and blue livery.

The first Corvette was a red/red convertible 427 Tri-Power grabbed right from the showroom and prepped as #29 (now #2). In addition to the various racing additions, it was also given an L88 engine. Because the new 1968 L88 wouldn't arrive in time for Daytona, Yenko built a parts car around a bare body and frame, and used a supplied L88 engine. This car ran as #30 at Daytona and is now restored as #4, its number at Sebring.

Ralph Morrison and the team had their sights set on competing in all three major endurance races that year: Daytona, Sebring, and Le Mans. The best finish at Daytona was from the #8 car, driven by Don Yenko and Dave Morgan, which placed 1st in the GT class and 10th overall, the same finish as the previous year. The other two cars finished 4th and 5th in the GT class and 25th and 27th overall, rounding out the effort.

For the 1968 Sebring 12-hour race, the '67 was replaced by the new '68 factory L88 Corvette and the three cars were given their now-recognized numbers 2, 3, and 4. While #2 and #4 received DNFs, the #3 car, which was the only factory L88 of the three 1968s, driven by Dave Morgan and Hap Sharp, secured a 1st-place GT-class finish and an incredible 6th-place overall finish.

With sights set on Le Mans, Don Yenko and Dave Morgan took

only one car to race at the Watkins Glen 6-hour race, where the car was crashed. Although the remaining two cars were invited to qualify at a two-month-delayed Le Mans, the Sunray DX team canceled the last showing for the 1968 season to concentrate on 1969. A 1969 season never happened because Sunray's merger with Sunoco led to the disbanding of the team. The last race in which a Sunray DX Corvette competed was Watkins Glen. The last full-blown effort with all three 1968 Corvettes was the 1968 Sebring 12-hour.

Where Are #9 and #4?

What happened to the five Sunray DX Corvettes? DX #9 had proved its mettle in France and was to be celebrated upon its return to the United States. However, it was soon stolen, repainted, and later recovered. The #4 Sebring car was carried over to Owens/Corning by

As is often the case, race cars changed hands regularly and were constantly upgraded, painted, and modified to suit the needs of the new owner. Since Tony Delorenzo and Jerry Thompson owned the #4 car, they moved to Owens Corning after Sunrail DX disbanded. Kevin is often asked why the car wasn't restored to its original Sunray DX livery. His answer is that the car was more successful with Owens/Corning, and race cars are the most valuable restored to their most successful trim.

drivers Tony DeLorenzo and Jerry Thompson. The other two '68s, including the one crashed at Watkins Glen, were presumably sold, losing their once-proud credentials in the process. The '67 #8 car with a red interior was presumably sold at that time as well.

The Hunt for #8

Monterey 1987 showed off some of the finest Chevrolets on the planet to honor the marque's 75 years in existence. Kevin was enjoying the field of Corvettes when he was struck by a particular car that he had never before seen in person: the 1967 factory L88 Le Mans car in its Sunray DX race trim. "I saw the Le Mans car, in red, white, and blue, and I thought it must be one of the prettiest cars I've ever seen in my entire life," Kevin says. "It was magnificent. I drooled over the car."

That particular Corvette was owned by Ed Mueller, a man who would soon become a dear friend, mentor, and customer of Kevin's. By this time, Kevin had just started his business, and he soon learned from Ed that to be the best, you had to go after the best. While doing work on the #9 Le Mans car, Kevin and Ed discussed the research and documentation that had been done. Ed mentioned that while searching through photos of his car, which has a black interior, he came across several photos of an identical car with a red interior and the number 8 on the door. To the casual observer, it appeared to be the same car, so Ed got in touch with Dick Guldstrand to ask him about the discrepancy. Guldstrand thought back past the many Corvette race cars he had been involved with over the years and recalled that there had been another L88 with the Sunray colors. He then said that the car was gone and couldn't be found.

Years later, Kevin and Ed had become close friends and in talks about the #8 car they had just assumed that it was a goner. There simply weren't any leads to the car's whereabouts or what happened to it after the dismemberment of the Sunray race team. The fabled red interior car didn't pop up again until Kevin was tracking down the John Paul L88 racer and was talking to racer and collector Tom Rynone from upstate New York. Casually, Kevin asked Rynone if he had owned any other L88s. He responded that he had owned one of the Sunray DX cars. Kevin's ears pricked up immediately.

"He took out his wallet and showed me a picture of the #8 car," Kevin remembers. "It was a DX car with a red interior! He said he sold the car to a guy named David Dempsey on Long Island, where I'm from. I said, wait a minute, I know David Dempsey; he's the president of the local Corvette club!"

Not only had Kevin scored his first and only lead on the missing #8 car, it was easy to track down David Dempsey. The car's history was now complete to a certain point, and it had not been destroyed. The car was purchased by Bob Luebbe in 1969, and he continued to race it competitively in its original Sunray DX trim. In 1970, Luebbe sold it to Dave Laughlin, who repainted it a different red, white, and blue trim and also continued to race it. Rynone bought it from Laughlin soon thereafter, raced it for a while, then sold it to Dempsey in 1974. Kevin learned all that in 1990; and a lot can happen to a racing Corvette in 16 years.

As soon as Kevin returned home from his visit with Tom Rynone, he began making phone calls and quickly tracked down David Dempsey. His first question: "You got a '67 Corvette?"

"Yeah."

"Is it a coupe with a red interior?"

"Yeah; I've owned that car for years."

"Is it for sale?"

"Yeah, it's for sale."

"Can I come over tonight?"

"Sure."

Kevin still had a financial partner involved with his business at the time, so he called him and told him he thought he might have found the DX car with the red interior. The partner was skeptical, quickly pointing out that Dick Guldstrand had said it was destroyed. "Well, they *believe* it was destroyed," Kevin responded. "But you can't take anyone's word for it. We have to go look at the car."

Although he trusted the information from Tom Rynone, Kevin had to prove to himself and his partner that this was the correct car. Because race cars rarely have much of their original telltale components, identifying one comes down to a process of elimination and mathematical likelihood.

"Picture this," Kevin began to explain to his partner. "The cars were white on top with a red hood stripe and blue on the sides. The car had a red interior, which means it originally could have been black, red, or white. If I'm a betting man, that car was probably a factory white car with a red hood stripe and red interior. All they had to do was paint the sides blue."

His partner agreed with this reasoning and they went to see the car.

"We got to David's house and we went in his garage. The car had flares and it was all customized. I looked underneath the dash at the trim tag and sure enough, it was a white car with red vinyl interior. I saw evidence of body indentations, I saw evidence of frame modifications, and I could see that it was a heater-delete car from the firewall. Out of 22,490 cars that were produced in 1967, you know how many cars were no heater? 35 cars. Out of 35 cars, they only made 20 L88s. So the odds were with me that if it was a heater-delete car, and it appeared to be a big-block, it was probably an L88."

Kevin looked at his partner, then turned back to Dempsey and asked, "What do you want for the car?"

His price was $19,000, but it didn't matter; Kevin just as quickly responded that they would take the car. He had $2,000 in his pocket for a deposit. But on the eve of one of the greatest discoveries in the Corvette hobby, there was a hitch. There was a couple who had been talking with Dempsey for the past year about purchasing it.

"Well, then, how come they don't own it?" Kevin asked. "I'm here to buy it. I'm here to give you a deposit tonight and I'll be back tomorrow with the money. You told me the car was for sale."

But being a man of his word, Dempsey had to give the couple the first option to buy the car. Kevin was losing his patience. "If they had first crack at it, they should have bought it. Look, I'm gonna be real nice. I'll give you $25,000 for the car. That's $6,000 more in your pocket."

Dempsey struggled to turn down the offer, but he repeated that he had to give the couple a call first. Kevin couldn't let that phone call happen. "Listen to me, this is business. If they wanted the car from the beginning they should've bought it like I did within 15 minutes of being here."

At this point, Kevin's partner interjects and asks if he could speak to him outside for a second. "No, not really," Kevin replied, feeling his easy, local deal starting to slip away.

"I didn't want to talk," Kevin says. "I wanted to make the deal happen. I was going to buy the car on Ed Mueller's behalf, figuring that if I could get the car for him, he'd give me the restoration in return. That's what I wanted, that's my business. That car, specifically, would help our reputation. Then my partner grabs and says, 'Excuse me, David. I want to talk to my partner.'

"My partner grabbed me and asked, 'What are you doing?'

"I said, 'If we leave this garage, we're going to lose this car. I'm gonna go back in there and offer him $30,000 for the car!'"

His partner disagreed, saying they would surely get the car for $25,000. Kevin said simply, "No, we're not. We're going to lose the car."

But his partner remained defiant and said they were staying at $25,000. Even at that number, Dempsey refused to sell until he consulted with the couple. Kevin and his partner argued all the way back to the shop. When he got home, Kevin called Dempsey back and offered him the $30,000 and pleaded not to sell the car to the couple. Sure enough, the couple had agreed to the higher price of $25,000 and had bought the car.

"I was devastated," Kevin says. "The car was sold. Son of a gun. I told my partner we had lost the car, and he said, 'Oh well, there will be other ones.' I was so upset I decided to go after all the other Sunray DX cars, because by now I had found out there were three '68s."

The Hunt for #2

After doing his research on the remaining unfound DX racers, Kevin hired the services of David Reisner to help track them down. They found the #2 car first, which had been owned and raced by a dentist in California. Although he didn't want to sell at first, thinking that the car was famous because of his successes with it, Kevin was able to score a deal on behalf of a client. The #2 was special in its own right. When Don Yenko ordered a 1968 L88, he was told that it wouldn't arrive in time for Daytona. So, he took a brand-new red-on-red '68 435-hp convertible off the showroom floor and converted it into the Sunray DX racer. As part of the conversion, he dropped in a factory L88 engine and campaigned the car as #29 alongside Peter Revson at Daytona.

After the Sunray DX team disbanded, Don Yenko continued to race this car and even won an SCCA Midwest title. "This was Don Yenko's personal car!" Kevin says. "But what's really amazing about that car is that I found a picture of them scraping off the window sticker. I was able to read the VIN number off the window sticker in the picture! But it gets better. . . .

"It gets better because I was tracing back some of the owners of the car, and found that one of the owners was a German guy in Key West,

Florida. He still had the original invoice for the car, but he didn't want to give it up. Probably 15 years goes by, the guy dies, and I call up his daughter and ask if he had any photographs or documents. She said yes, so I bought all the stuff. I was able to reunite the paperwork with the #2 car, so now that car is documented to the Nth degree. All the provenance history and the original invoice. Not only did he buy that car, he bought the '67 DX car and the DX flatbed truck."

After the successful find of the #2 Sunray DX car, Kevin and his team did a full-blown restoration and it currently resides in a private collection. It was the only Corvette that Pedro Rodriguez drove with Don Yenko.

Sunray DX #2 was being raced by a dentist in California when Kevin identified it as the car that received a DNF at Sebring in 1968. Although the dentist thought the car was famous because of his success, it was actually because it was raced by Don Yenko personally for a couple years. Years after finding the car, Kevin was able to secure tons of original documents and photographs from the family of a previous owner, completing the provenance history on the car. As you can see, a car of this magnitude hitting the auction block draws quite a crowd. Bidding went to $1.3 million, but the owner wanted more.

The Hunt for #3

Kevin then set his sights on the missing Sunray DX #3 car. Again, David Reisner's investigative prowess came into play and he was able to trace the car once again to upstate New York, and the town of Dresden, not far from Watkins Glen. Unlike other finds, this one stopped abruptly with the third owner of the car, Joe Sears, who had purchased it in 1973 and, after a short racing stint, stored it away in his barn.

However, Sears had no interest in selling. When he bought the car in 1973 from the Quaker State team, the first thing he did was sand it down to paint it white, his favorite Corvette color. As he disassembled the car, he discovered a DX decal underneath the wiper door. He knew he had one of the old DX racers.

"In six to eight months of him telling me the car wasn't for sale over the phone, we started to develop a nice relationship," Kevin says. "I didn't pressure him at all."

Luck stepped in that August as Sears drove by his local car dealership and saw a white 1988 Anniversary Corvette sitting on the lot. Those white-painted wheels and clean, white interior stood out to him as something that he and his wife would love. And being only a few years old at the time, it was a car that could be reliably enjoyed every day of the week. He called Kevin with a deal: If Kevin would buy Mrs. Sears that white '88, which would cost $15,000, he would give him the DX car.

"Obviously I couldn't get the money out of my pocket fast enough. That was August 1991; I remember it like it was yesterday."

Joe Sears had but one request, that Kevin would be the owner of the car. He had enjoyed their talks and friendship over the previous months, and it was important to him that Kevin would be the caretaker. This posed a minor problem, as Kevin had already discussed buying it for Ed Mueller who was excited to add it to his collection, after an expert Corvette Repair restoration, of course.

"Ed, I've got some good news and some bad news," Kevin said when he called his friend after learning of Joe Sears's request. "The good news is that I can get the car for 15 grand."

Mueller was ecstatic. "That's great news, Kevin! Let's take it, and I'll give you the restoration. What's the bad news?"

"The bad news," Kevin began, "is that I'd like to buy it for myself."

Ed Mueller immediately supported his friend's decision, and even offered to spend the day picking it up with him, using his trailer

Unlike other racing Corvettes at the time, the Sunray DX cars used a stock rearview mirror and lacked oversize fender flares, giving it a surprisingly showroom silhouette.

because Kevin didn't have one at the time.

Just a few months later, Mueller pulled the same game on Kevin when he owned the Penske Grand Sport #2 and was considering Corvette Repair for the complete restoration. He called up Kevin one day and said, "I got good news and bad news. The good news is I made $300,000 today."

"That's unbelievable!" Kevin responded. "What's the bad news?"

"I just sold the Grand Sport and you're not getting the restoration," he laughed.

When they went to roll the car out of the barn, they

Like his other L88 Corvette finds, DX #3 also earned a spot on the cover of* Corvette News*, making it an excellent target to hunt down while also adding to the provenance of the special car.

Even without paint or body, it's obvious that DX #3 is a purpose-built racer. Unlike its other third generation stablemates, #3 was born as an L88 Corvette directly from the factory. Thanks to Corvette Repair's cutaway restoration, Corvette enthusiasts were able to see just what made this car so special.

discovered the car was almost entirely complete. All the original body panels were there as well as the original interior, gauges, console, seat, and roll bar.

"It was an incredible find. We could see the history as we stripped the paint. We could see the green Quaker State colors. We could see the red, white, and blue DX colors. We looked at a picture of the Yenko crest badge on the hood bulge from 1968. We looked at the car and it had got the original badge mounting holes with the 427 badge mounting holes next to it. We looked at a picture from 1968 then looked at the car; all the comparisons were there. It had all the telltale signs."

The initial restoration saw #3 turned into a driveable chassis, following the success of the *Bounty Hunter* driveable chassis. It was first displayed at Carlisle in 1998. Ralph Morrison Jr. and his wife were there for the unveiling of the car as well as several members of the crew team. Morrison supplied Kevin with all his original photos and videos of the car to be included in its documentation.

The next transition for #3 turned it into a cutaway car. That version was essentially a complete car, except that the donor body was cut perfectly down the middle. Look at it from the right side and you'd see DX #3 in its original form, but look at it from the left and you'd see a driveable chassis. In 2000, the car was completed in its entirety and displayed for the first time at the Corvette Museum.

Shortly after, Kevin sold it to a collector in a package deal with *the Rebel* #57 car and the VV Cooke #80 car for $350,000 each, a record at the time. After being raced for a while, it was sold to Irwin Kroiz of Philadelphia, who commissioned Corvette Repair to freshen it up to the condition of its original restoration. Kroiz currently owns the car and has preserved it in its 1968 livery.

Kevin Mackay on His Early L88 Finds

David Reisner and I found some of the most important cars. We were just picking them out because nobody cared about race cars back then. Everyone wanted numbers-matching cars. So we went after these race cars because I figured that most of them started life as something special with a heavy-duty engine, heavy-duty brakes, heavy-duty transmission, heavy-duty radiator, etc. For race teams then, it was cheaper to buy a factory L88 car than to try to build one.

I couldn't afford a documented, original, factory L88 car. I couldn't afford it when a guy had one for sale, but I could certainly buy one without the guy knowing what he had. So most of these cars weren't worth anything because they didn't have the original engines and they didn't have documentation with them. But I had the documentation for them and I started doing backward searches, forward searches, putting the pieces of the puzzle together. I started to connect the dots and complete the circle. That's what I was doing. I was persistent and I had a lot of assistance from friends.

I blew through every Corvette book and read all the race entry lists from Sebring, Daytona, and Le Mans. The most important race in America is Sebring, the second most important is Daytona, but the most important race ever for Corvette is probably Le Mans. That's the most prestigious race. So I figured cars had to be pretty special if they were racing in those three races. They had to have all the heavy-duty options, so that's what I went after. And nobody really cared.

Then we started promoting these cars and now they're becoming extremely collectible, quite desirable, and very sought after. If you have a factory L88 car with racing history *and* it won, that raises the value tremendously. It's like a good piece of real estate or a good stock. And we were just picking these cars up like taking candy from a baby. Nobody really had any interest in them at the time.

CHAPTER 7

1969 See-Through L88

“THE COOLEST THING I EVER PULLED OVER”

In the early 1990s, not too long after Corvette Repair first popped onto the scene, Kevin had quickly become a well-respected Corvette expert, restorer, and ambassador of the hobby. He received a call from a young body man and painter who had just started working in the industry but wanted to work for Corvette Repair under Kevin’s tutelage.

Richard lived in New Jersey and Kevin turned him down at first, not thinking he would like the long commute to Long Island. But Richard ("We called him Itchy Ritchie because he was scratching all the time," Kevin laughs) pressed on, saying that the Valley Stream–based shop was the best place to be and he wanted to learn from the best. Kevin liked his attitude and hired him.

Over the course of a year and half, "Itchy" Ritchie (probably something to do with working on fiberglass all day) turned out some beautiful work in the shop before leaving to start his own business working on cars. Kevin admired the young man's drive, and the two continued to keep in touch. Occasionally, Ritchie called with a question or part that had him stumped and Kevin was always glad to help him.

One day in 1999, Ritchie called and said that a local guy in New Jersey was selling an L88 Corvette, and since he knew Kevin was heavily into big-blocks and L88s, he set him up with it first. The car was sitting in a machine shop in Piscataway, New Jersey, and the owner hadn't advertised it yet. Kevin grabbed some cash and drove his truck out to Piscataway that night to look at the black/black coupe, his favorite color combination. Within two minutes he sized up the car and negotiated a deal. The gas tank sticker proved that it was indeed a real sidepipe L88.

Not only was the sidepipe option a rare find, black was the rarest color for a Corvette from 1963 to 1969. Only 1,059 black cars were made out of the nearly 39,000 sold in 1969. That year also happened to be the last that black Corvettes were offered; that's how few were sold. Although the owner was asking $28,000 for the car, Kevin's $1,000 cash deposit came at the right time, and he gave it to him for $22,000. It was a steal of a deal for a complete L88, especially with the options it had. Kevin chalks it up to being at the right place at the right time and being ready with cash. Even though the owner knew it was an L88, Kevin doesn't think he really understood how special of a car it was.

The see-through cars done by Corvette Repair not only show the inner workings of a Corvette but the painstaking craftsmanship usually hidden under the body panels. The only bit of fiberglass on the car is the rear panel that holds the license plate, taillights, and Corvette lettering. (Photo Courtesy Bill Erdman)

Two days later, Kevin and a friend picked up the car on his flatbed and brought it back to his home garage. This one was his to keep. He admired the small but precious collection he had built over the past decade. Four factory L88s now sat in his garage: the Sunray DX #3, the VV Cooke #80, and of course, *the Rebel* #57. But they were all race cars that couldn't be driven on the street, and so the black/black sidepipe car was the perfect addition.

See-Through Transformation

Once restored to a highly detailed rolling chassis, Kevin looked at it and decided to do something with it that no one had ever done before. He would turn it into a see-through car, fully equipped and driveable, leaving off nothing but the fiberglass body panels. But first it would have to be taken apart. While removing the shag carpeting, which looked more suited to a house in a 1970s horror movie, he found the name Andy written on the inside bottom of the carpet. Andy turned out to be the car's second owner, who painted it white and added headers to the engine. Kevin is still at work tracking down the complete ownership history of the car.

To mount everything necessary to make the car functional, he needed to bolt a metal birdcage to the chassis. All Corvette birdcages are painted with a green rust inhibitor, as are the headlight doors and any other metal pieces on the car. All the bumpers and bracketry were attached to the frame and items such as emblems and marker lights could be rigged up to float exactly where they appeared on a stock C3 Corvette.

Kevin gathered his staff and told them that they needed another idea to promote the business. Actions speak louder than words, he always says, and the concept was to build a perfectly restored and detailed see-through car. They laughed at him until he started to walk around the car and explain his vision. Soon, they start throwing out ideas on how to make the car fully operational without losing the spirit of the build. It didn't take the crew long to become excited about the challenge and start making headway.

As the concept came to life, one of the guys had the idea to mount the emblems on thin metal brake tubing so that they appear to be floating in midair. Another figured out that by mounting the metal headlight and taillight support panels, the headlights and taillights could be well supported and fully functional. The puzzle came together fluidly.

As the DOT-mandated bits and pieces went on, Kevin looked at it and pointed out that with a pair of front bumpers, the car would actually be completely street legal. He had been a New York State inspector prior to opening Corvette Repair and knew that there was nothing in the inspection rulebook regarding body panels. As long as everything was operational (horn, wipers, lights, brakes, suspension, and fluid tanks), the car should pass.

The entire dash was put back in the car with all its gauges and equipment. Both seats were reinstalled over a see-through plastic floorpan, and once the electrical harness, horn relay, and alternator were set up, they got the car running. Kevin trailered it to the local inspector who asked, "What do you want to do with this?"

"I want the car inspected," Kevin replied. The shop operator pointed out that the car had no body panels, possibly expecting Kevin to smack his forward and say that he knew they were forgetting something. Instead, Kevin simply informed him that nowhere in the rulebook did it say a car without body panels couldn't be inspected.

If you were a cop you'd probably pull this "car" over, too. Believe it or not, this 1969 L88 Corvette is 100-percent street legal and 100-percent functional. That green paint on the metal headlight doors and birdcage is a special primer that Chevrolet uses to prevent rust. This car's color is actually black. (Photo Courtesy Bill Erdman)

The operator agreed, and the car passed.

The See-Through L88 made its first appearance at the 2005 NCRS regional meet in Orlando, Florida, upon completion. The showgoers swarmed the car. No one had ever seen anything like it before. Not only was it an educational work of art, it was entirely street legal! The creation was featured on the cover of the NCRS *Restorer* magazine and featured in other outlets as well.

"It's been my calling card since 2005," Kevin says. "We had done this before with the cutaway car and the sideways car, so I knew that we had a niche here. No one else could do what we did when it when it comes to marketing their business. My dad always told me that there are a lot of good salespeople out there, but if you can come up with an idea that no one's ever come up with before, people will remember that."

In addition to being Corvette Repair's "calling card" at events nationwide, it was the only street-legal L88 in Kevin's garage, and he still took it to the street on occasion. Traffic literally stopped in the middle of the road to watch Kevin and his see-through Corvette drive by.

His ultimate test came when he was going approximately 25 mph one day in the car when he saw red and blue lights flash behind him. He was excited. *Here we go, this is my test,* he thought. He had his insurance card, registration, and driver's license at the ready. His seat belt was on and he was sure to signal as he was being pulled over.

"What are you doing?" came the voice of the police officer towering above him.

"I'm sorry, Officer, am I breaking the law?" Kevin asked politely before handing over his credentials on request. The officer returned to the squad car to run the information and then came back to Kevin, this time with a smile on his face.

"This is the coolest thing I've ever pulled over. I can't give you a ticket, you're obeying the law. The car is insured, you have a license, and your background check came up clean. In fact, would you mind if I take a picture of the car?"

"He was so nice to me, it was unbelievable," Kevin remembers the experience fondly, having been happy himself to have succeeded in his attempt to build a street-legal see-through Corvette. "He probably saw the car and thought, 'What the hell is this damn maniac doing out on the street with this thing?' After he took a picture he said 'Have a wonderful day,' and that was it."

CHAPTER 8

1960 Briggs Cunningham #3

THE QUEST FOR THE FIRST LE MANS CLASS-WINNING CORVETTE

When it comes to American racing facilities, names like Daytona, Indianapolis, and Sebring carry equity. And those tracks have all seen their fair share of legendary Corvettes take the checkered flag. But on a global scale, one racetrack reigns supreme: Le Mans.

Perhaps the most challenging 24-hour race of them all, fitting because it was the first, the 24 Hours of Le Mans is the ultimate test of any racing machine. The mechanical endurance required of a car is beyond what any race car can handle, and only specialized cars with thousands of hours of development can compete. Even then, the world's best still regularly succumb to the treacherous combination of street and track driving.

America's first foray into the distinctly European affair occurred in 1950 when top builder and racer Briggs Cunningham II developed a pair of Cadillacs, one a stock-bodied Coupe de Ville and the other a prototype, to compete. They finished 10th and 11th overall, and it cemented Cunningham as the first American driver to race an American car at Le Mans.

For the next five years, Cunningham competed at Le Mans with his own marque, Cunningham, built in West Palm Beach, Florida. Without a win, and the production cars remaining unprofitable, he raced his own car at Le Mans for the last time in 1955.

In 1960, Briggs Cunningham, who owned a Jaguar distributor at the time, returned to Le Mans in a huge way, fielding three specially prepared 1960 Corvettes and one Jaguar with the best drivers of the day behind the wheels. In addition to another Corvette fielded by the Camoradi team, these were the first Corvettes to compete at Le Mans.

The Cunningham Corvettes were painted white with blue racing stripes, the official color combination for American entries in international racing, and had blue interiors. They were originally ordered with 290-hp 283-ci fuel-injection engines and 4-speed transmissions; they came with Posi-Traction, heavy-duty brakes and steering, removable hardtop only, 24-gallon fuel tank, and radio-delete package.

Once at the Cunningham race shop, the team turned the race-ready Corvettes into Le Mans competitors. Stewart Warner gauges were installed into specially made dash plates and the 24-gallon fuel tanks were replaced by 37-gallon race tanks with quick-release Halibrand

All three Cunningham Corvettes use different color headlight covers: red, white, and blue. Roof lights were also red, white, and blue. The #3 car uses the red covers (as you can see here), the #2 car uses blue covers, and the #1 car ran with white covers.

fuel caps. Halibrand knockoff wheels and Firestone racing tires were added along with Lucas brake lights and additional running lights. Koni shocks and an additional front sway bar shored up the cars' chassis and likely made the lightweight aircraft jump seats that much more uncomfortable for the 24-hour drive.

The rear windows on the hardtops were modified with a sliding center window to relieve heat from inside the cockpit; a duct from the driver-side bumper routed fresh air through the driver's footwell. In the likely event of rain, which occurred often at the 1960 Le Mans, the right-side windshield wiper arm was moved to the center to prevent a potential interlocking of the wipers and blinding the driver.

The exhaust systems were modified to what's called a Sebring exhaust, which exits in front of the rear wheels through specially made splash pans. It's not a sidepipe configuration because the pipe itself still runs under the chassis. To keep the brakes running as cool as possible during each of the 8.365-mile laps, ducts run from the grated grille to the brakes.

The #3 car, driven by John Fitch and Bob Grossman, was the only Cunningham Corvette to finish the race. The #1 car crashed after

Those dark gray Halibrand knockoff wheels and black tires not only looked mean on the Cunningham race cars, they allowed for faster pit stops in addition to the reduced weight over the stock steel wheels. The side-exit exhaust fit right in with the race package.

Although much of the dash is factory original, you can tell that this car was set up for racing with the gauges, switches, and easily removable steering wheel. The car also uses special racing seats.

three hours, and the #2 car lost an engine after 20 hours. Toward the end of the race, after achieving a high position of seventh overall, the #3 engine also overheated, which caused a massive coolant loss. Because the Le Mans rule book states that fluids can only be added at specified 25-lap intervals, the #3 limped back into the pits after every lap to cool down. Finally, the team manager packed the engine bay with dry ice from the team's catering tent to cool the hot V-8 long enough to finish the race. It worked. Bob Grossman took the car across the finish line in a miraculous eighth-place finish, behind a line of seven straight Ferraris.

This was still a win for the #3 team, which placed first in the Big Bore GT Class, the best finish for a Corvette at Le Mans for the next 40 years! It wasn't until the venerable, factory-backed #63 C5-R finished first in the GTS class did Corvette make it back to world's most revered podium. Following the race, the Cunningham cars were returned to their original street-legal trims and sold off to fund the next wave of racers. All that was left of these pioneer American heroes were the many pictures taken over the course of 24 hours in France and newspaper and magazine clippings.

The Quest

Kevin Mackay had at this time been working on his first customer, and mentor, Ed Mueller's cars for several years before "Eddie" (as Kevin affectionately called him), sent over his 1967 L88 Le Mans racer. The #9 car, in its blue and white livery with a red racing stripe culminating at the tip of the classic Stinger hood is what Kevin refers to as "the holy grail, the best of the best," when it comes to Corvette race cars. Along with the car came Ed's complete documentation that he had personally collected and researched.

"I was looking at the scrapbooks," Kevin says, "and I saw a letter that he wrote to Le Mans, in French. He got back the car's serial number and all the entry lists and inspection sheets from Le Mans. I asked, 'Ed, how the hell did you get this stuff?'"

As many in the collector hobby have learned over the years, sometimes all you have to do is ask. Ed had simply heard that the Le Mans organization kept detailed records dating back to the beginning, and after acquiring the #9 car, he wrote asking for copies. The wheels spun immediately in Kevin's head, "I wondered if you could do that for all of the early cars that went to Le Mans. Ed wasn't sure; he said he was only interested in his car when he first wrote."

After speaking with Ed, Kevin opened the scrapbook again to see just what kind of information had been obtained. "I thought 'If there's this kind of documentation for the 1967 Corvette, maybe there's something for the 1960 Corvettes.' They were the first effort going to Le Mans. I started doing more research on the Cunningham cars and the Camoradi car."

Armed with a pen and paper, Kevin wrote to Le Mans early in 1992 in search of information on the quartet of 1960 Corvette race cars. No response. He then hired private investigator David Reisner out of Bristol, Connecticut.

"It turned out that all I had to do was write another letter," Kevin says. In French. He had a French customer at the time whose wife was fluent in both French and English, and she wrote the second Le Mans letter. Reisner sent the letter, along with a bouquet of flowers. "Four or five months later, I received a faxed copy from David of all the serial numbers of the Corvettes that raced at Le Mans in 1960. I had the holy grail of VIN numbers in my hand on this piece of paper. I was blown away."

It is tough to tell just from looking at it that his cherry-red-on-red 1960 Corvette was once raced at Le Mans as part of the Briggs Cunningham team. Cunningham led the first Corvette campaign at the French competition. It's a beautiful car alright but worth just a little more as the #3 Cunningham racer. Yes, that's John Fitch riding in the passenger seat.

At the time, in 1993, the only known 1960 Le Mans racer was the #2 car owned by Michael Pillsbury. Kevin decided to run the VINs anyway, a simple task in the days before identity theft and cyber warfare. He got two hits back immediately. The #1 car was located in Tampa Bay, Florida, owned by Jerry L. Moore. The #3 car was in St. Louis, owned by James Walsh. Kevin went after the winning car first, and pored through St. Louis area phone books in search of James Walsh, owner of VIN 2538.

"We got ahold of him and he still has the car," Kevin remembers. "The problem is, he didn't want to sell it. It's like playing chess. Of course the last thing I want to say is Cunningham or Le Mans. I have to make a move without pushing them."

For seven years, Kevin sent James and his wife books and magazines that he thought they would enjoy. He sent a Christmas card every year, and called once a year around the holidays to send his best wishes for the coming year and to ask, "How ya doin', James? How's

Anytime Kevin discovers a major historical find, such as the Cunningham car, his standard procedure is to host a reveal party. Industry experts and press are invited to the unveiling to inspect the car in its as-found condition and authenticate it before a restoration. This way there's a record proving the car to be real. That's Kevin's father on the near left.

my car?" Every year he received the same response, "You're going to get the car, but right now I'm still enjoying it."

"We started a friendship over the car," Kevin says. "Never met him or his wife. One day I called to wish them a happy holidays, and his wife picks up the phone. She says, 'Kevin, my husband's back is just killing him. The car's just sitting in the garage, and I want him to get rid of it. Talk to him; maybe he'll sell you the car.'"

By this time, as the reputation of Corvette Repair and Kevin Mackay continued to grow in the Corvette world, Kevin had developed an incredible friendship with Chip Miller, creator of Corvettes at Carlisle, and his son, Lance. Chip knew that Kevin was on to one of the Cunningham cars and admitted to him that the 1960 Cunningham racers were his favorite cars of all time. He said that if Kevin would allow him to be the owner of the car, Corvette Repair would receive the commission for the complete restoration.

As a shock to Chip, Kevin immediately told him that he would give him the car for whatever he paid for it. There was another race car on Kevin's radar that he liked even more, a car that we now know as the 1966 Penske Development L88, except that he couldn't afford both of them. He told Chip, "We're the best of friends, we'll have the two best cars on the planet. I'll get the Cunningham car for you and I'll get the Penske car for myself."

"One night I checked the voice recording at my house. This is before cell phone days. It's James Walsh. He said, 'I talked to my wife and I promised you that if I ever sold the car, you'd get first crack at it. I'm going to sell you the car.'"

This was at one o'clock on a Sunday morning.

"Guess what I did? I called Chip's phone. It rang twice. He picked up and said, 'Hello? Did you get me the car?' I said, 'I got you the car. How the hell did you know it was me?' 'Who else would call me at one o'clock in the morning? It had to be you!'"

Chip bought the car and had it shipped to Corvette Repair for what's known as an autopsy in the collector car hobby. Leading experts from all over the country ventured to Long Island to determine exactly what he and Chip had actually bought. A car of this magnitude deserved an unveiling of epic proportions. Timed to occur on Chip Miller's 58th birthday, Kevin and Chip invited Corvette experts, GM employees, collectors, magazine editors, friends, and the two original drivers, John Fitch and Bob Grossman, to see the car in person when the announcement was made. In front of everyone, Kevin carefully stripped the paint on the passenger-side fender to reveal the original, undamaged 1960 body and confirm the car to be the actual Briggs Cunningham #3 that won its class.

A Dream Realized

With the car confirmed, Kevin and the Corvette Repair team initiated what was one of their most daunting restorations yet, totaling 3,750 man-hours. Many of the unique racing parts had to be fabricated from scratch, and even something as seemingly simple as the hood pins cost thousands of dollars to have made. Most of the fabrication work was done in-house. Chip was very hands-on with the project, sourcing items including the seats and wheels himself.

Mid-restoration, the Cunningham #3 car was featured in a body-over-chassis display at the 2001 Corvettes at Carlisle so that attendees could see the painstaking detail that went into every inch of the car and wouldn't be seen upon completion. With the project completed in 2002, Kevin and Chip initiated a full tour circuit that started at Meadow Brook Concours d'Elegance in Detroit where it won best in class. Then they took it to the NCRS National Convention held in Monterey, California, where it was first previewed for the revered American Heritage award. While also in Monterey that August, the car was displayed in the Chevrolet tent at Monterey Historics and in the special display area of the Pebble Beach Concours d'Elegance. It ended up earning an NCRS American Heritage Award, which was given the following year at the NCRS national meet in Hershey, Pennsylvania.

This one car, because of its huge significance as not only being one of the first Corvettes to race at Le Mans, but its title as class winner, brought more publicity and excitement to Corvette Repair than any other car up to that time.

But Chip Miller had a special goal in mind for the Cunningham racer: He wanted to bring it to Le Mans in 2010 to mark the 50th anniversary of its first appearance on the French streets. It was his dream, his life's passion, and part of it included taking original driver John Fitch with him to pair the first successful American Sports car with the first successful American driver in international racing. That dream might have died with Chip's passing in 2004 if it weren't for his son, Lance, who bore his father's torch and kept the dream alive.

In 2010, Lance arranged to have the car shipped to France, where it was the guest of honor for the entirety of that year's Le Mans festivities. It was showcased at the Le Mans Museum before the race and in the Corvette Corral during racing events. On Saturday morning, before the race, and with 92-year-old John Fitch behind the wheel and Lance Miller riding shotgun, the 1960 Cunningham #3 Corvette led a parade of 50 Le Mans Corvettes around the track. That moment marked the culmination of Chip Miller's legacy, the posthumous pinnacle of a lifetime of passion for Corvettes.

Throughout Lance Miller's journey of taking his father's Corvette from the show circuit to the racing circuit, director Michael Brown produced a film documenting the experience. It features interviews with Kevin, John Fitch, Lance Miller, and others in addition to coverage of the events leading up to the final Le Mans lap in 2010. It premiered at the historic Carlisle Theater on May 6, 2011, with more than 500 enthusiasts showing up in Chip's hometown to be a part of the event that started in 1960 with Briggs Cunningham, carried through by Kevin and Chip in the 1990s, and completed in 2010 by Lance. The automotive odyssey was then forever enshrined for future generations in Michael Brown's *The Quest*.

When Kevin unveiled the restored #3 car at Corvettes at Carlisle, original driver John Fitch was there to be reunited with his old car. Here he is pictured between Kevin and Lance Miller.

CHAPTER 9

1966 Roger Penske Development L88

THE HOLY GRAIL

After having retired from his racing career in 1965 to concentrate on his new Chevrolet dealership and budding businesses, Roger Penske quickly got the bug to go racing again. This time, he wanted to be the man behind the operation, not behind the wheel. Because he had just purchased George McKean Chevrolet and turned it into Roger Penske Chevrolet in Philadelphia, Pennsylvania, the choice of race car was obvious. It had to be a Corvette.

General Motors had pulled out of factory race development again in 1963, but not before Zora Arkus-Duntov could develop five special lightweight, high-powered Corvettes called the Grand Sports. Plans were made to build 125 others for homologation purposes, but once GM brass caught wind of the plan, they pulled the plug. It was clear to Arkus-Duntov that he couldn't build the car he wanted to compete against the factory-backed Shelby Cobras that were eating Corvettes for breakfast on tracks all over the country. He couldn't build a car, but he could build an engine.

Development of the Mark II engine, a 427-ci big-block started toward the end of 1962, originally for use in the 1963 Z06 Mickey Thompson Corvettes being developed. Soon after, a Mark IV program took off that turned the 427 into a fully race-prepared engine, which we now associate with Regular Production Option L88. One such Mark IV was installed in a Grand Sport and raced at the 1965 12 Hours of Sebring for the first time. After that running, General Motors continued to develop the Mark IV in secret.

As 1966 rolled around, General Motors engineered the Mark IV 427 engine as the big-block option for Corvettes instead of the 396 available the year before. Any privateers who wanted to go racing chose this engine package, with 425 stated horsepower, and the regular delete options. There was no race-prep package available from the dealer. However, the Mark IV engine had proved itself and was ready to hit the track on a full scale. Arkus-Duntov engaged a limited run of these engines to be installed in cars that were also given an entire suite of heavy-duty race options and factory deletes. He reached out to 1960 *Sports Illustrated* SCCA Driver of the Year Roger Penske, whom he knew was in the early stages of putting a team together, and offered one of them to him for the 1966 season, starting with the high-profile races of Daytona and Sebring.

Arkus-Duntov believed this to be the perfect time to test the potential of the factory-built L88 and potentially put it into widespread use in the future. Although the Grand Sports struggled to compete against the mid-engine Ferraris, Porsches, and Fords, an L88-powered

The 1966 Penske racer is truly a sight to behold with its blue and yellow trim and experimental performance parts throughout. This is its current restored state, and the livery in which it won its class at Sebring in 1966.

The cover of Corvette News is reserved for the most important Corvettes, and the Roger Penske L88 Development Coupe is no exception. Although the image was taken at high speed and is a bit blurry, the car's livery featuring yellow side pipes, wheels, and Sunoco logo is clearly visible and provides another piece of evidence as to the car's history.

Corvette could certainly make waves against other front-engine production cars in the GT class.

Penske was on board, and called his friend Elmer Bradley, vice president of marketing for Sun Oil Company, about sponsorship. Sunoco was in a development stage of its own in the form of Sunoco 260, a 103-octane racing fuel. What better way to promote their racing fuel and cement themselves as L88 experts than by becoming involved with the first development L88 race car?

Unlike the previous run of Grand Sports, L88 Corvettes started life at the St. Louis assembly plant. GM engineering sent a special Mark IV engine to the St. Louis assembly plant to be installed in the car right from the assembly line and sent a second Mark IV to TRACO Engineering, a popular race-prep shop in Culver City, California. The term L88 first appears in a document from a meeting between Chevrolet and Sunoco on January 10, 1966.

In addition to the regular heavy-duty race options and factory deletes, what has come to be termed "the developmental coupe" also sported a prototype cowl-induction hood and prototype 2.73:1 Posi-Traction rear end. Only three such hoods were made at that time, two of which were put on Grand Sports, with the third being installed on this car at the St. Louis plant. A 1965 grille was fitted in place of the stock 1966 grille because it was lighter. The car was picked up at the St. Louis plant by Dick Guldstrand painted Rally Red and with a black interior. It was cold on the mid-January day he picked it up, and the race car had no automatic or manual choke on the carburetor. The factory workers had a hard time trying to start the car, and they pushed it to the side until Guldstrand showed up and had to pour fuel down the carburetor to get it to fire. He was also offered a blanket to keep him warm on the drive to Penske's Philadelphia-based shop in the heater-delete car.

Kevin spoke to Dick Guldstrand about the car. He relayed another funny story about the drive back to Penske Chevrolet. Because the car only had a couple of gallons of fuel in it on delivery, he had to stop at a nearby gas station to fill it up. The kid attending the pumps began loading the Corvette up on Sunoco 260 fuel and started to look a little nervous when the meter hit 20 gallons. At 25 gallons he stops to look under the car for leaking fuel and, finding none, continued to fill the tank. At 30 gallons he stops again, entirely perplexed, and asks Guldstrand what was happening.

"The kid couldn't believe it!" Kevin says. "Dick had to tell him that the car had an optional fuel tank that took 36 gallons."

For Daytona, the car kept its factory red paint scheme and wore the number 6. It originally showed up with wide aluminum fender flares, but tech inspectors required their removal to run the car in the stock production GT class. The night before qualifying, the TRACO L88 engine that had been built was flown in by a company called Flying Tigers and installed in place of the development L88. The Developmental Coupe was one of the fastest cars ever in qualifying thanks to the 540-hp V-8 and drivers Dick Guldstrand, Ben Moore, and George Wintersteen.

In the middle of the night, Wintersteen crashed the coupe into a slow-moving Triumph, knocking off the front end. He was able to limp it into the pits, but with the front section ripped off and the radiator leaking, the chances of getting back into the race looked poor. Two strokes of luck occurred in the pits: The first was that a spectator happened to have a big-block '66 in the parking lot. Penske's mechanics ran over to the car and began removing the radiator when the owner, Bruce Barron, who had been sleeping inside the car, jumped out and began yelling at the crew. Roger Penske told him what it was for and Barron approved, on the condition that he would perform the work. There was still another problem, however, in that race officials would have to black flag the car for not having any headlights. This wasn't just so that the driver could see, but so it would be visible to other cars. Bill Preston, from Sunoco's development department, came to the rescue, as he happened to have two

In its first race at Daytona in 1966, the front end of the Penske L88 Corvette got ripped off in a crash. You can just barely make out the flashlights taped to the fenders, which allowed the car to complete the race. (Photo Courtesy Kevin Mackay Collection)

Roger Penske's first race car on the trailer and ready to compete at Sebring, where it went on to take first in class. You can see the special hood that resembles a 1966 427 hood but doesn't have vents in the side. (Photo Courtesy Kevin Mackay Collection)

heavy-duty six-cell flashlights in the trunk of his car. The flashlights were duct-taped to what remained of the fenders, and the fiberglass was strung together with piano wire to keep it from breaking apart under heavy wind force.

Guldstrand got in the car once repairs were completed, still under the cover of darkness, and hit the track. The flashlights were useless; he couldn't see anything and returned to the pits. An irate Roger Penske went up to the car and yelled at him to get back out on the track. When Guldstrand informed him that he couldn't see anything, Penske told him to catch up to another car and follow its taillights around the track. He found a pair of red taillights that were traveling at a competitive pace and stayed right behind those taillights, passing car after car, throughout this entire portion of the race. As daylight broke, it turned out he was following the Ferrari team car, which competed in the fastest prototype class! Not only did this help the team break the GT-class record and secure a first-in-class finish at Daytona, it finished a remarkable 12th overall. Even with a major accident and time out for repairs, it finished 27 laps and four places ahead of its nearest GT competitor.

Following the remarkable success at Daytona, Sunoco requested that the car be painted its corporate colors of Sunoco Blue and yellow for Sebring, where it also wore the number 9. At Sebring, with no accidents, the Roger Penske Corvette won its class and finished

The "Prova" license plate on the Penske racer is a joke made at the expense of its Ferrari competitors. **Prova** ***in Italian means "prototype," and the Ferrari racers were referred to by the name Prova followed by a number. The Grand Sport wore "Prova XP1" and the developmental coupe wore "XP2."***

9th overall, tying the record as the highest-ever finish for a Corvette. The #9 Penske Corvette is also credited with being the first car to pull away from the starting line that year, even though drivers had to run from across the track and both enter and start their cars as part of the race. The Roger Penske Developmental L88 Coupe goes down in history as the only Mid-Year Corvette to win back to back at Daytona and Sebring in the same year.

The Chase

Kevin Mackay was at the Malcolm Konner Chevrolet show in 1983 when a Nassau Blue, totally modified 1966 Corvette coupe pulled in. The car was outfitted with fender flares, modern Camaro IROC wheels, and a special hood he hadn't seen before. He could tell by looking inside that it was a tanker and would surely have a story behind it.

"I didn't know what the hell it was!" he says.

He asked the owner about it and was told it was a '66 L88 that was once part of the Roger Penske team. "I never heard of that before in my life," Kevin remembers. "I know they came out in 1967 but not 1966. I was just blown away when he told me that."

The car was for sale for $135,000, an unheard-of amount of money for any Corvette in 1983, especially when '67 L88s were going for about $25,000. Kevin's friend and future customer Ed Mueller suggested, "Well, go find another '66 L88."

Although the Penske Corvette is oftentimes mistaken for one of the Grand Sports because of its coloring and racing equipment, when shown side by side the difference becomes clear.

"I just followed that car," Kevin says. "I remember taking pictures of the tags, and I kept an eye on it." The owner did get his money for the car a couple of years later when collector Gene Schiavone bought it to vintage race in addition to Grand Sport #1, which was the matching Penske team car now immortalized as #10. Schiavone raced them and showed them as a pair. Kevin ran into the car again at an NCRS regional meet in Mystic, Connecticut, in the late 1980s.

"I was just foaming at the mouth at that car. He told himself, 'One day, if I could win the lottery, I gotta have this car.'"

In the mid-1990s, major collector Dale Phelan went to Schiavone's residence after seeing the Grand Sport advertised for sale in *Hemmings Motor News* for $1.3 million. The Grand Sport by then had become too valuable for him to race anymore, and he was afraid he would kill himself in it or destroy the car. At that point, no Corvette had sold for more than $1 million. As Phelan looked over the Grand Sport, he noticed another Corvette next to it, under a cover. It bore the striking silhouette of a mid-year coupe. "What's under the cover?" he asked.

Schiavone pulled off the cover to reveal a matching Sunoco Blue and yellow Corvette that also had "Roger Penske Chevrolet" written on the fender. He had treated the car to a professional restoration to its '66 Sebring trim after initially buying it. Dick Guldstrand still had a race shop in California, and, after being sent the car to confirm its authenticity, was awarded the restoration. At the time, he also upgraded it with a dry sump and modern safety measures for racing.

This one wasn't for sale because Schiavone still enjoyed vintage racing it. And he raced it hard; the car showed 13,000 rough miles on the odometer. Phelan was instantly taken aback by the beauty of

FOR THE RESTORATION
AND PRESERVATION OF CORVETTES

Great Cars & Great Friends

SHIPPING DATA REPORT

Subject to the General Conditions listed on the reverse side, National Corvette Restorers Society, Inc. confirms the following information exists in the GM shipping data records for the 1966 Corvette with vehicle identification number 194376S110556.

The GM official Production Date was 1/10/1966

The original delivery dealer was Dealer code 487 in zone 15.

The name and Address for the Dealer was.

Penske-McKean Chevrolet
Philadelphia, PA

Thank you for using the NCRS Historic Document Services.

Roy Sinor
NCRS National Judging Chairman

November 18, 2010

A Shipping Data Report like this one is available to NCRS members to help trace the history of their Corvettes. Knowing the original delivery location can provide further evidence of a car's likely origin. The fact that this '66 was shipped to Penske-McKean Chevrolet further proves that it is the original Penske race car. Some cars show up as being shipped to Engineering, meaning they were used for GM testing and development.

the '66 and decided he wanted that one instead. Although Schiavone would have rather sold the more expensive Grand Sport, he had to sell one of them, and he estimated the value to be about half that of a Grand Sport. Phelan ended up paying a rumored $670,000 for it, and got to keep $630,000 in his bank account. He liked the history of the Daytona/Sebring winner even better and guessed that the prototype L88 was probably rarer than a Grand Sport anyway. He bought it and continued to race it.

Kevin's First Million-Dollar Sale

While the Penske Developmental Coupe was being raced and changing hands, and increasing in value, Kevin and his Corvette Repair team had developed an impressive collection of C3 L88 racers that consisted of the 1968 Sunray DX #3, the 1969 *Rebel* #57, and the 1969 VV Cooke #80. The DX and *Rebel* cars are what he still considers the best '68 and the best '69 on the planet. In 2000, after nearly a decade spent finding, restoring, and showing them, he received a call from a broker in Seattle saying that someone wanted to buy all three of them.

The cars weren't for sale at any price and Kevin didn't have any desire to sell them. The broker was persistent: "Mr. Mackay, we're willing to give you more money for those cars than you'll ever dream

This is what $1.05 million worth of Corvettes looked like in 2000. Kevin positioned the stunningly prepared cars perfectly in his garage. **The Rebel** ***and Sunray DX cars were fully restored while the VV Cooke car remained in its as-raced condition. What a sight this must have been for the buyer's inspector!***

of. Name your price."

"Well, it's going to be over a million dollars," he replied, thinking he could throw off the broker and scare him away.

"How much over a million?" he asked.

"I won't be greedy," came Kevin's response, "I'll take $350,000 a piece, that's $1.05 million." The broker was interested and asked to be sent some information. Kevin put together a 101-page binder and overnighted it to the West Coast with the reminder that if he didn't get his price he'd keep them. He knew they'd end up being worth that in the near future.

After two to three weeks of not hearing anything, Kevin started to become annoyed and thought he was being played in some type of scam. He called the broker and told him the cars weren't for sale anymore and he didn't appreciate the game that was being played. The broker calmed him down and said the buyer was away on business, but that he was blown away by the documentation and photographs. He asked that Kevin bear with him for just a couple more weeks.

A call came through just a week later. "We're going to come out tomorrow and look at the cars." They were sending a fellow restorer, a Cobra and race car expert, to gauge the quality of the restorations and confirm the validity of the cars. Kevin set up his garage perfectly with the documentation laid out on tables and the cars positioned just right to make the greatest first impression.

"I told him that if you look at these three cars, they are the best of the best. They were all on the cover of *Corvette News,* they were all factory L88s, and they were all painted red, white, and blue." He still didn't want to sell the cars, but he knew that the kind of money being offered to him would change his life.

His friend Chip Miller, co-founder of Carlisle Events, once again stepped in with valuable insight. "Kevin, that kind of money in your account could change your life. You worked your ass off all these years, and guess what? If you sell these cars, you can buy whatever you want. I know the car you keep talking about and I know you can't afford it."

Kevin decided right then that he would sell the cars and go after his dream car, the Roger Penske Developmental L88 Coupe.

After looking over the cars, the restorer simply said, "Mr. Mackay, we'll take the cars." And then handed him a check for $50,000. The rest would be wired into his account the following day.

"They were going to wire a million dollars into my account,"

Kevin remembers. "I said, 'S**t! I'm going to be a millionaire!'" It was something he thought he would never say, and most certainly thought would never happened. He knew this was a turning point in his life, and he wanted someone close to him to share it with.

On his way to the bank the next day to oversee the transfer, he stopped by his father's house. "My father used to call me a grease monkey," he says. "'You're never going to make it in life being a mechanic, you're never going to do anything.'" Kevin just wanted to work on Corvettes; money was always secondary to the passion. Parents tend not to understand that.

"Where are we going?" his father asked after being picked up by surprise.

"We're going to the bank. I want you to experience this with me. Don't say nothing, Pop, just listen and let me talk. I got a big surprise for you."

"So I went to the bank that I've been at since I was 15 years old and had a paper route. I never had much money because any money I made I put right back into the business. We got there and I said, 'I'm getting some money transferred into my account.' They asked me how much and I said, 'A million dollars.'"

Kevin's father turned to him and shouted in disbelief, "A million dollars! You're wasting my time!"

The bank manager had to come out to verify the transfer because everyone there thought Kevin was joking. He was dressed in his usual oil- and paint-stained old clothes as he had just come from the shop. The manager asked if he had just won the lottery to which Kevin replied that he had sold three cars and that if nobody believed him he would take his business elsewhere.

His father looked at him again and asked, "You sold the DX car? You sold *the Rebel* car? And the VV Cooke racer? For a million dollars? Those s**tboxes? Who would give you that much money for those cars? It has to be a scam."

"Well, Pop, we're about to find out."

Kevin had to fly to a show in Chicago later that afternoon and asked the bank manager to call him once the money went through. The bank was closing at 3:00 that afternoon, and by 2:30, he still hadn't received a call. His father came by to take him to the airport, so they stopped at the bank on the way, only 15 minutes before its set to close for the day.

At this point, Kevin began to think that the whole thing might actually be a setup. His father might be right about the deal being a scam. They got to the bank and asked for the manager to fill them in.

Finally, the manager came over and apologized for not calling; the day was extremely busy. "Mr. Mackay, congratulations, you just became a millionaire. The money is in your account."

"My father couldn't believe it; he was flipping out," Kevin remembers. "I was so proud that day because I didn't think it would ever happen. I was also sad in a way because those cars were a piece of me; the research and the hunting and getting everyone together. Those cars were a big part of my life. But there was one car that I wanted more than anything, and that's the Penske racer. Now that I had a million dollars in the bank, I didn't even care; I wanted that car more than the money."

The Dream Comes True

"The money was burning a hole in my pocket. I was single at the time, I had no kids, I didn't need the money. That's the car I wanted and it's not the quantity, it's the quality. I had been studying it since 1983; I knew all about the car. I said that if that car comes up for sale, which it never did since it was never advertised, I would buy it."

Buying a car that isn't for sale is a difficult business, but it's oftentimes the way many of the best automobiles on the planet change hands. Kevin reached out to his good friend Franz Estereicher who knew Dale Phelan well. Using an intermediary who's a friend of both parties ensures a level of fairness in delicate dealings. Estereicher had one request of Kevin: He wanted to own the car for a day. It turned out that Kevin had come in at the right time, as Phelan had gotten tired of racing it. The car had a few fender benders and showed battle scars all over. It was perfect for Kevin since he would want to tear down every nut and bolt on the car and restore it himself anyway. Estereicher bought the car and the following day, sold it to Kevin.

He was ecstatic, and as soon as the Developmental Coupe showed up at Corvette Repair, Kevin began taking stock of the originality. It was all there. The headlight covers, door lights, window reinforcements, header pipe mounting holes, dash, gauges, and switches were all original. It even came with the original 36-gallon fuel tank that had stayed with the car even after being converted to a fuel cell.

"We took that car all the way down when I got it. We put almost 3,000 man-hours into that car; I wanted it perfect. I didn't want to race the car, I just wanted to preserve the history; that's all I cared about. I wanted to bring it back as close as I could to the way it raced at Sebring, winning its class in 1966. The car went right down to bare glass and we did everything all over again."

The car re-debuted at the Monterey Historic Races in 2002. It went on to be displayed at Meadow Brook and it won an American Heritage Award from the NCRS. Dick Guldstrand was there in addition to the documentation to talk about the car and his initial involvement with it. He had spectators and judges in disbelief when he told the flashlight story from Daytona.

In 2016, Kevin attended an awards dinner at the Corning Factory Museum in upstate New York with his good friend Irwin Kroiz, who also owned the Penske Camaro. He knew Roger Penske would be in attendance and brought a complete binder of photos and documentation with him. As soon as Penske walked into the room, Kevin knew he had to get to him before a crowd developed wanting pictures and handshakes.

He walked up to him with an 8x10 photo pulled from the binder and said, "Mr. Penske, my name's Kevin Mackay and I own your first born." Penske looked at him and repeated the statement as a question. Kevin showed him the picture and the binder, and Penske invited him over to a table to go through the binder.

They spent 20 minutes at the function going through the binder as a large circle of people gathered around them, taking pictures of Roger Penske seeing his first race car for the first time since it left his possession, just over 50 years since it won at Sebring. After he signed Kevin's glove box door, "All the best, Roger Penske," Kevin and Irwin invited him to keep the books that they had prepared. Penske was speechless.

"I told him, 'I figured you'd like to have it to show your grandkids and your family where you started.'"

Eight hours after exchanging contact information that night, both Kevin and Irwin had personal emails from Roger Penske thanking them for the books and looking forward to seeing the cars in person in the future.

"I was blown away," Kevin recalls. "The guy was absolutely amazing. I couldn't believe he spent that much time with us. See, you always remember your roots, no matter how successful, how smart you are, how much money you make. You always remember where you come from."

CHAPTER 10

1965 4,310-Mile Convertible

"WHAT COLOR TOP DOES IT HAVE?"

By Kevin Mackay

There was a doctor, a neck and head surgeon, whose car I worked on, and it took him three or four years to decide where to take his car. He decided to bring it to me eventually, but before he sent it down from his home in upstate New York he asked that I come up to see the car and meet him. He always called me Mr. Mackay, and I could tell by the way he spoke that he was a very unique individual.

I went to his house, which was very well groomed, everything was in place. I walked in the door, and before I was allowed to go into the house I had to take off my shoes. So I took off my shoes and left them on the doormat. All his floors were high-polished mahogany wood. I thought he was in the Marines; the house was absolutely spotless.

He said, "I want you to come into my bedroom first." I look at the guy. He's serious. So I went into his bedroom, he opened this big cabinet and pulled out a three-ring binder. It's got every piece of documentation, every receipt, all his research, everything you can think of including letters written to General Motors when the guy was 21 years old. He bought a green with black leather 1965 Corvette with fuel injection, whitewalls, knock-offs, and a 4-speed. Everything. Every piece of documentation, even gas receipts were in the binder. The car had 4,310 original miles and had its original tires. I was completely blown away.

I said, "I'd like to see the car now, and call me Kevin." He said he has to call me Mr. Mackay. Okay Doc, no problem. So we went in the garage. He said, "Mr. Mackay, go get your shoes, carry them through the house, then sit here on this bench and put them on and we'll go in the garage."

I got my shoes, put them on, followed him into the garage, and I saw the car's all covered up. I said, "Let me help you take the cover off."

He said, "Mr. Mackay, don't touch the car cover. I'll take it off."

I looked at him and said, "Doc, you want me to work on the car, I gotta help you take the cover off. You don't want me to touch anything, but how am I going to work on the car?"

He said, "I'm sorry; you're right."

It turned out that he had three covers on the car. Three car covers on one car! It took him probably 15 minutes to take them off. He folded those car covers like you would fold an American flag at a funeral.

After the third car cover came off, and we folded it like an American flag, I looked at the car. He had handkerchiefs wrapped around the wiper blades so the blades wouldn't touch the glass, with three rubber bands wrapped around each one. He had handkerchiefs wrapped around the door handles. It's the most magnificent original car I'd ever seen in my life. It was like a time capsule.

I went to open the door and he yelled at me. "Mr. Mackay, you can't go over the door handle; your fingernails will scratch the paint. You have to go under the door handle and then push the button. But be very careful, Mr. Mackay, I don't want any scratches on my car."

It was just amazing how he preserved this car. So I opened the passenger's door and looked inside. There weren't even creases in the leather. He said that the only person who ever sat in that car on the passenger's side was his mother . . . once. The seat was basically brand new. I went on the driver's side and opened the door, putting my hand underneath the door handle. I looked inside the car, there's not a pebble, there's not one piece of dirt on that carpet. The carpet was brand new. I looked at him and I said, "Doc, there's not even a wear-mark where your foot would be for the gas pedal."

"Mr. Mackay, you see the low mileage on the car? You see the inspection sticker on the car?" The inspection sticker was for 1972, but really the car hadn't been on the road since 1971.

He had owned the car for six years and only took it out in absolutely perfect weather. He never took that car out in the rain or snow, ever. If it was going to rain that day, he'd leave the car in the garage. With three car covers on it. I kept looking at the car and I was still just blown away.

He said, "Mr. Mackay, since the day I bought that car and brought it home, I always drove that car with my shoes off." Excuse me? "I would bring a paper bag with me. I'd take my shoes off and put them in a paper bag in the cargo area.

"One time, in the late 1960s, I was driving the car in New York and I know clearly in my head I went through a yellow light and I got pulled over. I almost got arrested. He told me to get out of the car, and I told him I wasn't getting out of the car because I had no shoes on.

"The cop said, 'Get out of the car.'

"I said, 'I'm not getting out of the car until I put my shoes on. I've got my shoes in the back.' But the cop was afraid I had a gun back there."

The cop realized soon that the guy was harmless, so he let him get out of the car in his stocking feet. He let him go in the paper bag to get his shoes and put them on before stepping into the street. The only person who's ever sat in the driver's seat was him. The only person who ever sat in the passenger's seat was his mother. The car had every option you can think of. It was amazing.

It had the optional hardtop mounted on it, so I asked him, "What color is the soft top?"

He said, "I have no idea."

I said, "Wait a minute, Doc. You bought this car brand new?"

"Yes, I bought it brand new, but I never had the hardtop off it. I have no idea what color the top is."

I said, "You gotta be kidding me."

Before the car left his facility, I had to sign a contract that the car had to be picked up in an enclosed trailer, which it was the following week. After my friend loaded the car in his trailer, the Doc drove all the way down to Long Island with it. Part of the agreement was that the car had to be on my lift the entire time, with three car covers on, and I couldn't take the car on the street ever. He'd come down every Saturday and clean the car.

He originally sent the car because it had all these plastic chrome bicycle looms and colored covers on the wiring harnesses and chrome parts in the engine. He wanted me to take all that off the car. He wanted me to dechrome the fuel injection unit, which we did. And half the chassis was painted with a neon yellow paint. He wanted that to be removed and he wanted us to put the correct asphalt black paint back on the car. That was the only thing not right on the car, and that's what really bothered him.

I said to him, "Doc, I gotta find out what color the soft top is. You gotta let me!"

I videotaped the opening of the soft top. We removed the hardtop and opened the rear deck. The soft top still had the white protective paper on it. The top hadn't been up since the car was manufactured in St. Louis in 1965. So you had a green car with black leather interior, and for a '65 Corvette, you had your choice of three soft top colors: black canvas, white canvas, or saddle canvas.

I was thinking green with black leather. A black top would be my guess. I was wrong. When we pulled the soft top up, it was saddle. Beautiful. The car was unbelievable. The soft top was brand spanking new. We took some heat guns to very carefully warm it. Then we creeped it up. It took a while because it was folded in there for more than 40 years. This was probably in the late 1980s or early 1990s when the car came into my shop.

He called me on a yearly basis when he started it. Maybe not for a couple of years now, but I'm assuming he's still around. I was just completely blown away by that car and the way he took care of things. This was the first and only time in all the years I've been doing this to open a brand-new soft top. He didn't even know the color of his top because he had never seen it.

It's amazing what's out there, and I'll guarantee that top has been down for the 27 years since I left it. The car's probably exactly the way it looked, with three car covers over it.

But now you know why the car was so extraordinary: The guy was such a perfectionist. He ordered that car out of Malcolm Konner Chevrolet in Paramus, New Jersey. He still has the car today. He'll deny it, but he's got the car.

Now I'll tell you the best part of the story. We got kinda friendly with him. There was a 12-mile 1967 L88 that was in Seattle and I was talking to the doctor about it. He said, "You know, Kevin, that's a pretty rare car, but does it have the original engine?" I told him it didn't.

"Oh. You know I have a '67 L89 car, too."

I said, "Doc, what do you have?"

He said, "I'll deny it to anyone else, but I have a '67 L89 Corvette with 11.3 original miles on it."

I said, "Doc, I gotta see the car."

He said, "The car's at my mother's house in Florida. I'll deny it to everyone else, but I have every piece of paperwork. I've only ever changed the parking brake because it was seized in the rear brake rotor. Every option you can think of is on the car except the big tank."

I've been asking to see that car for 15 to 20 years. He won't show it to me. I haven't seen it yet, but I believe him. I believe him. He doesn't like talking about it. He also has a ZR-1 Corvette that he bought new in 1990; he's got no miles on that one either. He buys all his cars out of Malcolm Konner Chevrolet.

I'd say that '65, exactly the way it is, is worth half a million dollars. A restored fuel injection car would bring $150,000 to $200,000 done really well with the right paperwork.

I think the '67 is worth more than a million. A '67 L89 car? They only made 16 of them. Although they're not as desirable as an L88, those cars are bringing $450,000 to $550,000. But with 11.3 miles, totally original, original owner, with every piece of paper you can think of, plus the three car covers on top of it, that car's getting a million bucks at auction if not more.

CHAPTER 11

Kevin's Corvette Stories

By Kevin Mackay

Having spent 30-plus years in the Corvette business, Kevin Mackay has had some interesting experiences, some of which are so crazy that they can only be true. People have had close relationships with their cars since the dawn of motorized transportation, and those connections only intensify when the memory of a loved one is involved. Other connections are so bizarre that the only plausible explanation is fate. Although this is a book of Kevin's greatest Corvette finds, some of the most important cars he's worked on may not be worth very much monetarily, but to their owners, they're priceless. This collection of short stories includes just a few of them that stand out.
—Tyler Greenblatt

The Undertaker's Corvette

I got a call from a little old lady in the Hamptons whose husband bought her a car in 1965. It was a black/saddle automatic with every option and only 11,000 original miles. I went out there to look at it and it still had the original tires, the spare was never used, and it really only had 11,000 original miles. It was a really cool car. It had leather, every option, air conditioning, power steering, brakes, windows, two tops, all the paperwork.

I brought the car back, changed the fluids, threw a set of plugs in it, put air in the tires, and the damn thing ran like a top. Around the same time, a guy from Canada called me up and said, "I'm looking for an automatic small-block. Do you know of anything?"

I said, "You're not going to believe this. I got this one-owner, black with saddle automatic."

He asked if I would hold the car for him. I said, "The car's not advertised, but I have it, and if you don't buy it I'll keep it for myself. It's a cute little car." The guy came down, looked at the car, and we went for a ride. He loved the car.

"What kind of documentation does it have?" he asked.

I said, "It's got it all."

So the guy was going through the documentation, and he looked up at me, and said, "You're not going to believe this. I know the original owner of this car."

Although it was the wife's car, it was still under her husband's name. "I know this lady's husband."

I said, "How? You're in Canada."

"You know what I do for a living? I'm an undertaker. I buried the original owner of this car."

I said, "Come on, now." I looked at the guy like he was crazy.

He said, "Kevin, I'm telling you, I know this guy. I put the makeup on him, I changed him, I put him in his coffin. I'm telling you."

This woman's husband owned Sara Lee cakes, which has been around forever. I believe he died in Florida, but they had a wake and the funeral services, because he was originally from Canada, in Canada. So that's how this guy knew him.

So I called up the wife, "By the way, I have this guy next to me, and he says he knows your husband." I told her his name.

The lady said, "I know him. He kind of knows my husband because he buried my husband. That was the funeral parlor that we used."

So I gave the guy the phone, and he said to her, "I'll take your car."

So here's a guy, lives up in Canada, buries the original owner. You'd have a better chance of winning the lottery than having this story ever happen again. I was completely blown away; that was such a weird story. I tell ya, I was spooked.

He still has the car today, too. I was in Quebec doing a class for the local NCRS chapter not too long ago, and after I told this story, one guy said, "The guy's still got the car." He called him up and got him on the phone and he told the exact same story to the class.

1959 Life Saver Corvette

A gentleman called me up from upstate New York, this is going back 20 years now, and he asked, "Do you restore Corvettes? I was just on your website. I'm going to send you a car to do."

The guy was in the Westchester County area, so he sent the car to me. The car was hit in the right rear quarter panel, hit real hard. So it needed a whole rear clip. The car was all messed up, too, but it did have the engine in it. The car was really just a shell, a basket case.

It probably seemed like a great deal to Dr. Rick Kole when he was gifted a 1959 Corvette by a grateful patient. Understandably, when Kevin saw it for the first time, he immediately informed Dr. Kole that it would cost a lot less to buy one that's already been restored.

I told the guy who delivered it, "Don't even take it off the truck; leave it alone. Let me talk to the owner to see if he's sure he wants to spend that kind of money on the car."

I told him, "A restoration is not cheap, okay? You're going to spend well over 100 grand on this. You can buy one for 50 to 60 grand. Why would you want to do this to the car?"

He told me, "Kevin, listen to me. I have the money; just do it. I don't care what it costs. I want it painted back to black, bring it back to stock. That's all you have to do."

I said, "I think you're making a mistake."

"I make a lot of money," he said, "I can afford it. Do it."

Okay! So he came down once a month to look at the car. It was coming together nicely and he kept paying all his bills. He paid me instantly. He said, "You're doing a great job. I can't wait to see it done." This went on for about a year. It came out beautifully.

When it was all done, he came to the shop, and I said, "Rick, I just don't understand why you would put this kind of money into this car."

He said, "Kevin, you don't understand how important this car is to me."

"Well, tell me the story."

"I'm an M.D. and I had a patient come into my office with dizzy spells, and he felt like he was going to throw up all the time. By the end of the day he'd feel a little better, but he'd been going to different doctors and nobody could figure out what he had.

"So he came into my place and I said, 'Do you have a garage attached to your house?'

"He said, 'What does that have to do with the dizzy spells and me feeling like I have to throw up all the time? What difference does it make?' He was getting aggravated now.

"Just answer the question."

"'Yes I do.'"

"Thank you. Now, do you work during the day?"

"'What does that have to do with anything?'"

"Answer the question."

"'Yes, I get up in the morning, I put a cup of coffee on, then I go in the garage and start up my car, let it run about 15 minutes to get it warmed up, then I go to work.'"

"I figured out what your problem is. You have carbon monoxide poisoning. That's why you're having dizzy spells. Just open the garage door, pull the car into the driveway, and let it run there. Let me know how you feel in a month.

"The guy comes back a month later and says, 'You're not going to believe this. I'm like a new man. No more dizzy spells, no more having to throw up, you saved my life. I've been like this for years!'"

The doc said, "I'm glad I was able to help you."

Now this doctor had a lot of classic car pictures in his office. The patient said, "Doc, I see you're really into cars."

"Oh yeah, I love all cars, especially muscle cars."

"You know something? You saved my life. I have a gift for you." He gave the doctor his 1959 Corvette, for free. The car was a complete basket case, smashed in the back. He had been in an accident with it and it was sitting in his backyard for years. The doctor was so taken back, and so moved by it, he was speechless.

The patient said, "My dream was to have this car restored, but I don't have the time or the funds. I'm just glad you could find out what my problem was. I hope this car gives you as much joy as it gave me."

The doc went online, did his research, found out about Corvette Repair, and he could not wait to get started on this project. From the

Yes, this is the same 1959 that Dr. Kole had brought in to Corvette Repair that looked more like a donor car than a restoration candidate. The Corvette Repair crew patched in new fiberglass panels and sources all the correct parts to complete the job and fulfill Dr. Kole's wishes.

day he shipped the car until he paid his final bill, he was so excited about that car. As soon as he got the finished car, he was going to drive it over to the patient to show him.

He said, "You know, Kevin, I was so moved and touched by this guy, so I just can't wait to show him the car."

And now I could understand why the guy would spend that kind of money. It was just about doing the right thing.

9/11 Corvettes

After 9/11, a guy came in with a 1976 Corvette. It's probably a $3,000 to $4,000 car. I told him the frame was shot on it. "Well, get me another frame." I got him another frame, took the body off, took the undercarriage off the car. We redid the brake lines, fuel lines, and hoses to make it safe. The guy probably spent 30 to 40 grand on it. He used to come down with his dad. He'd always say, "Aw, this is great. This is great."

So I gave him the final bill and I asked, "Why would you want to put this kind of money into this car?"

He said, "You don't understand how important this car is to me."

I said, "I'd love to hear your story."

"I lost my brother on 9/11. He was in the building when it collapsed. The last time we were together we decided that we were going to buy an old Corvette and drive it, race it, whatever. So in memory of him, I wanted to rebuild this car. This car was the last memory I have of him.

"We found it in a local paper and we saw the car, and we kept thinking about it. The following day, he died. About a month later, the same car was in the same paper. I had to buy it because that was the last thing I did with my brother. That's why I put this kind of money into this car. It was the last thing we did together."

I told him I understood completely. He said, "Thank you, thank you, thank you. I'm going to enjoy this car for the rest of my life."

His father was crying, he was crying, I was almost crying. It was very touching.

Then, about three years later, which is four or five years ago now, a guy came in with a '64 Corvette convertible. The inspection sticker was dated 2001. The guy said, "Look, I need a battery. I need brakes. This used to be my dad's car. Can you get the car up and running? I want to drive it. My mom gave me the car."

The car had been sitting since 2001. So we went for a road test, we put new gas in it, and I showed him how to work the car. It was his dad's car for many years. He lost his father on 9/11 and the mother gave the car to her only son.

I got the creeps seeing the car and looking at the inspection sticker. The registration sticker said 2001, so the last guy who drove this car was his father. The car sat all these years after its owner died.

Those two stories really affected me with how precious life really is. I was happy to help make them smile after a loved one's death. It was cool being a part of that, to put a smile on their faces.

I haven't heard from them since, so the cars are probably parked and they take them out when they want to.

CHAPTER 12

Lucky Local Garage Finds

By Kevin Mackay

When it comes to hunting down important Corvettes, no one has a better record than Kevin Mackay. In all, he and his team of experts have found 13 lost L88 Corvettes in 30 years in addition to the dozens more non-L88 cars on top of that. Every now and then, he'll get a lead on a car that makes the whole thing look easy. Sometimes, it's a car that had been sitting for decades and the owner or descendant has finally decided to sell it. Other times, he gets a tip from a friend who's seen or heard of the car. Oftentimes, it turns out to be nothing or it's a car that Kevin has little interest in. But every now and then, it turns out to be a special car and, even better, it's located within walking distance of his home! These are two stories of the kinds of "barn finds" that every car enthusiast dreams of uncovering, finds that would make any of us "shake like a leaf" like when Kevin pulled the blue tarp of *the Rebel* Corvette. Barn-find Corvettes are still out there, and if anyone disagrees with you on that, tell them they're right. That's just one less person looking for them! —Tyler Greenblatt

1958 Garage Find

I got occasional calls from one guy over the years looking to sell me parts. Then all of a sudden I didn't hear from him for a while. Then he called me out of the blue one day and asked if I bought Corvettes. I told him, "I buy them if I can steal them, but I'm not in the buy and sell business." I asked him what he had.

"It's my grandfather's car," he told me. "He just passed away and I inherited it. It's been sitting in the garage since the 1970s and doesn't run. I got myself in a little trouble, I got arrested for armed robbery, so I was in jail for seven years. Now I have no money, I'm broke, so I have to sell it."

It turned out that he lived in Elmont, New York, which wasn't far from the shop. I said I could be over there in 30 minutes. So I ran over there and the car was a completely intact, dual-quad '58, silver blue with blue interior, hardtop on it, and there was crap all over the car from floor to ceiling. Lounge chairs, mattresses, junk.

The car'd been there for years, so it took me three or four hours to get everything out of the way. It had flat tires, so we winched it up on the truck and took it home. I think I bought the car for $10,000 in cash. I offered him five for it, but he said, "I'm not that stupid."

It was a pretty original car. I don't think his grandfather was the original owner, but I think his grandfather bought it from the original owner.

The car needed everything. It had mostly original paint, but the paint was shot on it. My plan was to keep it and make a hot rod out of it or something cool like that. Then a guy in Pennsylvania who buys and sells cars offered me $28,000 for it. He bought three cars from me in one shot. I think the guy still has it; he's going to restore it himself.

It just fell in my lap, and once in a while I get a car that does just that. It was probably 10 minutes away from my shop.

Who knows how many great classic Corvettes are sitting in barns and garages across the country. Kevin came upon this stunning blue '58 not too far from Corvette Repair and picked it up for a great price, too. You can call it a New York barn find!

It's easy to understand why the car hadn't been spotted and uncovered during all the years it sat. It was covered, and the garage is tucked way behind the house, away from view. Sometimes a clue like a cool old truck parked outside can mean something even cooler is hidden away.

1960 Gasser Garage Find

I had heard about this car from Gary "the Brush," a very well-respected pinstriper. He's still doing it actually, although he's got to be getting close to 70. He used to be the pinstriper for Joel Rosen from Motion Performance in the 1960s, so he knew a lot about the Long Island performance car scene at that time. He told me about an old gasser he knew of that had been sitting around forever in nearby Merrick, New York, which turned out to be walking distance from my home at the time.

So I got ahold of the owner and met him at the house to see the car. We opened the garage door and it was just amazing. It was painted a metallic tannish, brownish, goldish color and was literally just sitting there. A time capsule. It still had the original carpets and the original dash but the nose on the front was narrowed. The hardtop was with it when we found it; I like the look of a hardtop. It had a '68 Camaro 396 engine with headers and straight pipes sticking out the sides.

Originally it was a white/black fuel injection car that was bought from a used car lot in Queens in 1962. That's the owner who turned it into a drag car, so it's been a drag car since 1962. He didn't like the fuel injection, so he swapped engines with his buddy who had a Camaro. I saw the fuel injection emblems on it at first and couldn't believe it: The car was a real fuelie! He used to take it out to East Long Island, there's a dragstrip out there, but I think he did some street racing, too. There was a lot of street racing going on in the 1970s, but this car really wasn't practical for street use. You can pop wheelies on it all day long, it's so light in the front.

It's a local car, which means something to me, so I traced the ownership after I bought it. It turns out that I know some of the people who owned it. One of them was Bird, another pinstriper in the area. I bet he's still around. When he bought the car, he titled it under his brother's name because he had a better driving record. I guess his insurance was less because of that.

The two brothers don't talk now. Bird told me, "It was really my car, but legally it was my brother's car. I don't talk to him anymore because we had a big fight."

I was able to talk to both of them after I hunted down the brother who had it registered in his name. He said, "It's my brother's car; I just

The bronze/gold paint scheme on this gasser, along with the custom hood, leaves no doubt that this car is a true survivor!

did it for insurance purposes. Here's my brother's number. Don't tell him I gave it to you because we don't talk anymore."

I love getting people together with the car, and when I found this car I was so excited. I had never owned a gasser before, but I always wanted one. I like the look of the gasser. When I saw it, I just had to have it. It was in this area, it raced in Suffolk County, and it raced in Queens; it was just a local car that never left the state. The price was right; I think I had the business pay for it as a company car. I took it to all the local shows. That's where you want to take it to learn more of its history. Maybe someone remembered the car, remembered it on the street, or remembered it at the track.

I took it to the Muscle Car and Corvette Nationals in Chicago, where they have a "barn find" display area and it's one of the most popular things at the event. I also took the '62 drag car, and put them side by side. They both have original paint and it was crazy to see them together. They're just good, honest cars that haven't been touched in 50 years. The inspection sticker from 1965 was still on the windshield!

When I take the '60 gasser to a car show, people go crazy over it. And you can actually drive it; it's street legal but handles like crap because it's got that high front end. But that's period-correct 1960s.

The car just happened to be sitting in a garage all these years, abandoned. Thank God it was in the garage. I left it just the way it was. How many cars are out there like this that haven't been touched in more than 50 years? It wouldn't pay to restore the car back to stock. Putting that car back to stock would maybe bring $100,000 to $125,000, but you'd have more into it by restoring it. I think I paid $25,000 for the car, which was a fair price for a running car. I started it up right there. The right thing to do is to preserve the story, and that's what I paid for.

The car's currently not for sale. The best time to sell something is when you don't have to sell it. If I go to a show and someone asks if I want to sell it, I say, "Show me the money."

I get calls all the time from people wanting to sell me things, but most of the time it's a car from the 1980s or 1990s, a C4 or C5, which I have no interest in whatsoever. If it's from the 1950s or 1960s, then I listen. If it's a big-block, if it's got fuel injection, or if it's something rare, or has any kind of cool history then I have interest in it.

Sometimes people just give cars to me. "Get it out of here," they say. A guy gave me a '72 Corvette that was just sitting outside in his backyard. He asked if I had any interest in the car. I said, "Not really."

"What if I give it to you?"

"Well, then I'm definitely interested."

"Just pick it up and get it out of here," he said.

It's happened on three or four occasions.

After Hurricane Sandy, there were 15 or 16 cars that were literally totaled. The insurance companies were so overwhelmed they didn't even bother showing up. Long Island was like a war zone. We didn't have power for two or three weeks at the house. It was pretty scary. Owners just gave them to me, even though I didn't want them. I use them for parts or fiberglass.

Even though they're not the kind of cars he's usually known for, Kevin gets a kick out of showing off these survivor drag cars. They're just cool, old Corvettes that tell a story of a bygone era.

CHAPTER 13

1969 Baldwin-Motion Phase III

HOW PHIL SCHWARTZ GOT HIS FIRST CAR BACK

Few names play to all the senses of a Bowtie muscle car fanatic like Baldwin-Motion. Whether it's the unique look or unrivaled performance, Baldwin-Motion Chevrolets are Grade A when it comes to collectability for investors and enthusiasm among show goers. The hallowed name comes from a combination of Joel Rosen's Motion Performance and the nearby Baldwin Chevrolet. This Long Island, New York, tag team allowed customers to buy a super-high-performance car built by Motion as a brand-new car from Baldwin.

Rosen extended his tuner talents beyond muscle cars, however, finding some of his most enthusiastic customers in Corvette owners via a handful of different outlets. For custom shops in other parts of the country, and for those looking to tune Corvettes they already owned, Motion supplied most of its parts through a catalog. Another option was the Phase III, which retained the general stock appearance, except for the paint scheme and racing fuel cap, yet had all of the Motion performance work. But for collectors and Corvette lovers around the world, the one that stands out the most is the Baldwin-Motion Phase III GT.

The Phase III GT

The GT truly was its own automobile, highly distinguishable from showroom-stock Corvettes from every angle. The car's front clip and pop-up headlights were replaced with Monza-style headlights inset deep into the flared front fenders. Off-road (racing) sidepipes crept along the bottom of the rocker panels and dumped out just before the wide rear tires. The rear fenders also received a healthy dose of flaring to cover the wide race rubber. The rear end dumped the traditional pair of round taillights in favor for the three-bar setup from a Firebird.

The biggest, most instantly recognizable feature of a Phase III GT is the large, tilted rear window, which replaced the vertical, removable rear window that was sometimes difficult to see out of on stock coupes. The big window stretched the length of the defining C3 "Flying Buttress" B-pillars. This concept, which Corvette founding father Zora Arkus-Duntov reportedly loved and regretted that General Motors could not build, was actually done for functional reasons on this otherwise performance-oriented supercar.

Joel Rosen loved Corvettes, but the cargo space on a C3, even the coupe, was nearly unusable for anything more than local drives.

After 40 years of being apart, Phil and his first car were finally reunited. Kevin and the Corvette Repair team restored the Baldwin-Motion Phase III Corvette to exactly the way it was when Phil first bought it. If you look closely you can see that they even kept his Stewart Warner gauge on the wiper door.

Phil Schwartz was living every boy's fantasy in 1969 when his father bought him a brand-new Baldwin-Motion Phase III Corvette. He terrorized the streets of Long Island until he crashed headfirst into a parked car. Joel Rosen of Motion Performance swapped in his new Phase III GT front end, giving the car a unique look.

Rosen and his wife loved traveling with their Corvette and their dog, so in addition to the large, angled rear window, the GT was also hollowed out underneath it. Where the rear deck would be on a stock coupe, the GT was open underneath that big window, allowing for a massive improvement in carrying capacity like the C2s that had come before it.

Under the hood, later GTs sported a 454 LS6 and earlier ones mostly used 427s, both pumping out more than 500 hp. Every dragstrip upgrade was used, and for the $10,000-plus price tag, you could even get air conditioning!

It's believed that 12 Phase III GTs were built under the Baldwin-Motion moniker, although with the success of the catalog kit, there are many more lookalikes on the road today. Kevin restored a one-of-a-kind 1969 Phase III GT; it was the only one to be ordered with the standard Dodge Challenger fuel cap. For $15, every other GT customer opted for the Cobra Le Mans-style gas cap. That car is an NCRS American Heritage Award winner and is Muscle Car & Corvette Nationals Concours certified.

Of the original 12 produced, 5 remain unaccounted for, and may very well be driven regularly, with the owners under the impression they have one of the many catalog kits that were sold by Motion. The value on those cars doesn't differ much from their stock counterparts, but real Baldwin-Motion Phase III GTs have been known to fetch between $250,000 and $650,000.

"The Phase III GTs are the most desirable ones to a collector," Kevin says. "You just gotta get the right guy who's gotta have one. Some people say they could be worth three quarters of a million dollars, but I don't believe that.

"Once in a while you see one on eBay and it could be a real one or it could be one of those catalog cars."

That's not to say the "catalog cars" don't have any value. He puts those in the $100,000 to $125,000 range. All the Baldwin-Motion cars had regular VIN numbers, so there's no easy to way to visually tell whether or not someone's car is a real Baldwin-Motion. Running the info on the VIN through the GM Heritage Center would reveal the car's original dealership. If that pops up as Baldwin Chevrolet, there's a solid chance it's the real deal.

Of the five lost Phase III GTs, Kevin believes that at least two are still intact and somewhere on Long Island. One of them is supposedly a black-on-black car owned by the original owner. The other one is also believed to be an original-owner car, although its condition is unknown. Although Baldwin-Motion cars did end up all over the world, they were predominantly purchased by local customers and have likely gone through several New York area owners by now, with their original provenance having been lost along the way.

A Deal for Good Grades

Phil Schwartz was in high school when his father told him that if he got good grades and graduated honorably, he would buy him any car he wanted. Phil graduated in 1969, and true to his father's agreement, excelled with his grades and quickly traded his diploma for the latest car magazines in search of a car. Being from Long Island, the high-performance street machines coming out of Motion Performance in nearby Baldwin, New York, were local legends, and 18-year-old Phil decided that's what he wanted.

After speaking with his father and telling him that this is what he wanted, they went to Baldwin Chevrolet and ordered a 1969 Monaco Orange 427/435-hp Corvette with the Motion Phase III package.

The Baldwin-Motion Phase III Corvette parked safely in Phil's driveway after being repaired by Motion Performance. You can barely identify the GT front end when looking at it from the side.

This is a Baldwin-Motion Phase III GT restored by Corvette Repair. Only 12 were built and it's easy to see what makes them so special to collectors today. Unlike Phil's car, the GT features a completely reworked slanted rear window in addition to the Monza-style front end.

Phil ordered sidepipes and the special dual-disc clutch, which only 101 other buyers opted for that year, thinking he would be doing a lot of drag racing. The dual-disc clutch was only available on the high-horsepower Tri-Power cars. Phil also ordered luxury appointments including power windows, power brakes, leather interior, and just about every other available option. Once he got the car home, he installed a Stewart Warner fuel pressure gauge on the wiper door, right in front of the windshield.

Not long after taking delivery of the car, Phil was showing off by doing spin-outs in a local parking lot one night when he lost control and hit a parked car. He blew the entire nose off the car and returned to Motion Performance to have it fixed. Joel Rosen had just developed the Monza-style front end for the upcoming Phase III GT cars he was building and asked if Phil would like him to put that on his car instead. Phil thought that the single, open headlight conversion piece looked cool, as many young people did at the time, and let Motion Performance run with it.

Phil ended up meeting and dating his future wife (currently of 40 years) in the Baldwin-Motion Corvette before they were married and started a family. He traded the street racer for something a little more family friendly. Although he never saw his car again, he thought of it often, especially years later when his children had grown up and he became involved with Corvette collector cars.

Phil was one of Kevin's first customers in the 1980s, and from the first day they met he talked about his old Baldwin-Motion car. "Every time I saw him, he'd tell me about this car," Kevin says. "He'd say how nice it would be to find his old car, and he would go on and on. Now you can imagine hearing this for 30 years."

Kevin humored him as a friend and customer, but he had heard so many stories just like it over the years that he didn't pay Phil much mind. As Phil and Kevin became better and better friends, he started coming to the shop on Saturdays to talk Corvettes and check up on projects that were underway. One day, he pulled up to Corvette Repair especially excited about something. He walked right up to Kevin holding a picture of him and his friend from high school standing next to their cars. His friend was leaning against an orange Camaro, and, sure enough, Phil was leaning against a 1969 Phase III Corvette. Kevin ceded that Phil had been telling the truth all these years, and Phil once again told Kevin how much he wanted to get his old car back.

Short on Money

Just a few years later, Kevin was looking on eBay the way he usually does, when he noticed an auction for a 1969 Monaco Orange Phase III Corvette with a GT front end and sidepipes. The seller had a letter from Joel Rosen authenticating it as a true Motion Performance car. Kevin couldn't make out the interior from the photos or see if any of Phil's options were on the car.

He called Phil. "Phil, are you near a computer? You're not going to believe this, but there's a car that's the exact description of your car on eBay."

Phil hurried to a computer to look at the listing and 10 minutes later called Kevin back and exclaimed, "That's my car! That's my car!"

"Oh come on, Phil. How do you know that's your car; you can't see any of the options?"

"You see that gauge mounted on the wiper door outside the front windshield on the driver's side? That's a Stewart Warner fuel pressure gauge. I put that in myself. That's my freaking car!"

With Phil positive that it was his car, a simple call to the eBay seller could clarify some of the specifics. Kevin called and asked about some of the minor details on the car. First, he asked about the GT front end, even though the car was a regular Phase III. The seller told him that Joel Rosen authenticated it as being correctly done at Motion Performance. Next, Kevin asked what color the interior was.

"Black," came the response.

"Is it vinyl or leather?"

"Leather."

"Does the car have manual windows or power windows?"

"Power windows."

"Now I see that it has a gauge mounted on that wiper grille outside the windshield. What kind of gauge is that?"

"That's a Stewart Warner fuel pressure gauge."

The car was exactly the way Phil had been describing it all those years. The Buy It Now price on the car was $225,000, but Phil was only prepared to pay $100,000 for the car. Kevin told him that the seller wouldn't come down $125,000, but Phil insisted that he make the offer.

Kevin didn't even have a chance. When he called the seller back just 10 minutes after they had spoken, someone else had swooped in with a cash offer and bought the car.

"Phil was very upset," Kevin says. "He was freaking out, but I told him we wouldn't have been able to buy the car for $100,000 anyway. Of course, as the months go by, I hear about how he lost the car and he's just crushed, devastated."

Auction Surprise

Two more years go by, and Kevin was doing research on the Yenko Corvette online forum. There was an announcement about a big collection going to public auction in Connecticut. Supposedly the owner had a tax problem and the state repossessed his valuable classic cars. Sure enough, there was a 1969 Monaco Orange Motion Corvette with a Phase III GT nose. The car had been recently restored but they left the nose on, meaning that it had likely been authenticated by Joel Rosen as correct. It was Phil's car.

Kevin called his buddy. "Phil, I found your car again. It's going up at a no-reserve public auction in Connecticut. Phil, you've got to become a bidder!"

"When is it?" Phil asked.

"Next weekend," Kevin replied, to which Phil replied that he

Phil's first car as-found on eBay. It had obviously been sitting neglected for many years. Although Kevin was skeptical that this was really Phil's car without a deeper investigation, Phil knew it immediately by the little chrome Stewart Warner fuel pressure gauge that he installed himself on the wiper door.

couldn't make it because of a wedding he had to go to. "Well, then, you'll lose the car."

Phil told Mrs. Schwartz that he was not going to the wedding so that he could buy his old Corvette back. Let's just say she wasn't pleased with her husband.

Kevin and Phil took off from Long Island the following Saturday at 5 a.m. to drive to the auction in Connecticut. "Now here's a guy who has not seen this car since he was 19 years old. And here he is now in his 60s. You're talking 40 years. He's a nervous wreck.

"I told Phil that I couldn't go anywhere near the car because if I went near the car, people were going to think I was interested. And if they thought I was interested, they would think it was something special and they'd go crazy for it."

Phil couldn't relax, so Kevin suggested that they go to a nearby diner for some eggs and pancakes to wait for the auction to begin. Phil couldn't eat and he could barely drink a glass of water. He started to pace back and forth in the diner. We went back to the auction.

"Phil, we're not going to lose the car," Kevin told him. "Do you want to bid or should I?"

"I'm not bidding; I'm too sick to my stomach right now. I just want my car back. Kevin, please get me my car; whatever it takes. Just don't lose it."

"Okay, Phil, but if you're only going to $100,000, you're going to lose the car." Phil cleared Kevin to get him the car at any cost. The restoration was poorly done and the work appeared amateurish, but that didn't mean that the car couldn't potentially sell for standard Baldwin-Motion kind of money.

The bidding started, going slowly at first. $50,000, $60,000, $70,000. Kevin sat back and watched. The auction cracked $100,000 and at $125,000 nearly all the bidders dropped out. Kevin jumped in at $130,000. Every time he bid, another bidder was right there with him raising the stakes another $10,000. At $180,000, Kevin turned to Phil and asked him what to do. "Stay in. I don't care what it costs. Just get me that car!"

Kevin got up and walked over to the other bidder. "Look, do me a favor," he told him. "Put your hand down. You're not getting the car, okay?" But he wanted the car.

"Just put your hand down; we're going to buy the car. There's a reason for it." But the other bidder kept going. The price climbed over $200,000; Phil motioned to Kevin to stay in it and keep going.

Finally, the other bidder put his hand down and the auctioneer hammered the sale at $225,000. Phil won the bid. He could've bought it on eBay two years before for $225,000. But he finally got the car.

After Phil had received his keys and the title, Kevin walked up to the auctioneer and told him that he had an announcement to make. He told the crowd that the buyer of the Motion Corvette was the original owner of the car; the place erupted in applause. Phil ran up on stage and started bowing. He was in tears as he hugged Kevin and then hugged the car. He went to sit in his car and the emotions continued. "It was amazing," Kevin says.

Back to Original, Almost

The car had to be taken to Corvette Repair for a complete restoration back to the way Phil and his father picked it up from Baldwin Chevrolet in 1969, before the accident. Although Phil pointed out that he owned the car with the GT nose, Kevin told him that because the car was originally a regular Phase III, it had to be put back to that specification. Phil agreed, and trusted his friend's expertise.

As Kevin's crew took the car apart, they were continually shocked to be working on 18-year-old Phil's car. He checked the codes for power brakes and the dual disc clutch, which were correct, and even he couldn't believe that they had gotten the car back after all the years that had gone by.

Kevin had to source an original 3-barrel carburetor and Edelbrock manifold that would have come on the car originally, since they had long since been replaced. They needed to find special valve covers and wires, and a Mallory distributor, which were all part of the Motion package. Phil had upgraded the shifter to a Hurst T-handle originally, so Corvette Repair put that back in the car for him. Of course, they had the Stewart Warner fuel pressure gauge restored and put back on the car the way he had it. The original T-tops were never restored and were instead replaced with another set. They came with the sale of the car and now Phil has them on display with his collection, in their original paint, just as he got them back in 1969.

After the restoration was complete, they even took a picture of Phil with his car standing in the same position as the picture from 1970 when he was 19 years old. "To this day he's so attached to the car after it was missing for 40 years," Kevin says. "Phil was thinking about his dad and how his dad got him the car. It was a very emotional ride for him, but boy, you ought to have seen him when he first saw the car after we restored it. His stomach was in a knot, he didn't know what to say, he was speechless. And Phil is never speechless."

The Truth Comes Out

Although Phil enjoys showing the car locally, he and Kevin took it to the major national shows including the Muscle Car and Corvette Nationals in Chicago and an NCRS regional meet, which took place in Gettysburg. Old photographs of Phil accompanied the display, and he loved telling the 40-year tale to show attendees. At the Chicago show, Phil and his Corvette were reunited with Joel Rosen, who remembered Phil and his father first buying the car. He even signed it for him.

"Reminiscing with those two guys was hysterical," Kevin remembers. "Everything that Phil had told me was 100-percent true. A lot of people say they used to have this or that. Yeah, okay. But he shut me right up. He really did own this car. I was blown away. Phil had kept telling me to go find this car, but whenever I asked him for the name of the person he sold it to, he couldn't remember. We can either do a forward search or a backward search; that's how we find these cars. But when he told me about the Stewart Warner fuel pressure gauge, you can't make that up. It's like a fingerprint, and one fingerprint can change everything!"

Once the car was retired to regular use in Phil's collection, after completing the show circuit, Phil and Kevin went to a party in his old neighborhood with friends who remembered the car. They continued to fill in the puzzle pieces that Kevin likes to complete with every car that he works on. Over the years, he's learned that when a story is legitimate, all the pieces fall together perfectly. And when it's a scam, nothing fits or makes sense.

Kevin had to clear up with one of Phil's old friends whether or not Phil had been telling the truth about being fast with the car back in the day. "Oh, yeah," the friend responded, "Phil was the fast Jewish kid!"

How cool does Phil look leaning against his brand-new Corvette? He must have just gotten the car because it has the original front end and no Stewart Warner fuel pressure gauge. His buddy's Z/28 Camaro ain't half-bad either.

CHAPTER 14

1965 Fuel-Injected Tanker

SENTIMENTAL STREET

Objects from our past tend to have a way of bringing us closer to people, events, or special memories that we hold dear. Cars, Corvettes in particular, oftentimes are the epitome of such a phenomenon. Chuck Spielman, owner of Only Yesterday Classic Autos in San Diego, California, always dreamed of owning a car originally sold at his father's Chevrolet dealership. Maybe his father had signed the purchase order, or had even sold the car to a customer personally. Any car from the dealership would do, as it would provide that unique bond that Chuck needed to feel closer to his father.

Chuck Spielman had been a friend and client of Kevin's for many years and they often saw each other and chatted at the major shows throughout the year, such as the Pebble Beach and Amelia Island Concours. At one such meeting, in the mid-2000s, Chuck remarked to Kevin that his father used to own a Chevrolet dealership in New York. Being the proud, lifelong New Yorker that he is, Kevin was instantly intrigued as Chuck told him about his ongoing, yet unsuccessful, mission to find a car that came out of his father's dealership where he had worked for years.

"I always remembered that, and kept it in the back of my mind," Kevin says of the encounter.

Around 2010, Kevin learned of a 1965 big-tank Corvette residing in a collection, but it was not for sale. Tankers, as they're colloquially known in the Corvette hobby, are mid-year Corvettes fitted with RPO N03, a 36-gallon fuel tank generally meant for racing. As the second rarest option in 1965, only 41 cars were built with the $202.30 big-tank package out of the 23,563 total Corvettes. This particular tanker had black paint and a black vinyl interior, making it one of two (at the time, before Doug Fortune's black/black tanker was discovered in 2012) known black/black 1965 tankers. Unlike the Doug Fortune tanker, this one was equipped with fuel-injection; it was the last year for fuel injection and the 396 in the Corvette. Only 771 cars were produced with the $538 option.

"What makes the car so unusual," Kevin says, "is that four-wheel disc brakes were available in 1965, but this car had drum brakes on it. They only made 316 with drum brakes, which was a delete option." Someone could order a Corvette in 1965 with drum brakes by using option code J61, which gave a $64.50 credit. "This car had all the bells and whistles: fuel injection, big tank, but it's got drum brakes. It's a really oddball car."

Being the oddball car that it was, and finished in the classic black/black color scheme, Kevin had to have it. "I told the dealer that if

Unlike later big-block Corvettes that can be easily identified by their unique hood bulge, not a lot separates this high-performance '65 from its small-block brethren on the outside. What's under the hood is anything but ordinary. Only 771 cars were built with the fuel-injected small-block.

Underneath that black rear deck lies an N03 36-gallon fuel tank, making this Corvette one of only 41 Tankers built in 1965. Also of note on this '65 Corvette is the Z01 Comfort and Convenience Group package, which includes a No-Glare mirror and back-up lamps, which weren't standard until 1966. Most owners took this $16.15 option.

the car ever came up for sale, I would have great interest in it, either for myself, personally, or for a client." The dealer agreed to let Kevin know if he was ever able to convince the owner of more than 20 years to sell. With the first option to buy the unusual car secured, Kevin moved on to another project.

Finally, in the summer of 2016, Kevin received the long-awaited phone call from the dealer regarding the "oddball" '65 tanker. Although it would be easy to get excited about such a call, Kevin had to perform his standard due diligence on the car, which consisted of requesting and examining its documentation. Among the documents was an NCRS file, available to any member for $40, which listed the original dealership as Spielman Motor Car Company in Brooklyn, New York.

Kevin recognized the name immediately and thought back to his conversation with Chuck several years earlier. "I thought, 'Spielman? Oh my god! It's got to be Chuck's father's dealership; it's got to be!'" Only having Chuck's work number, he called and left a voice mail with the incredible news. The call was never returned, so Kevin tried again, this time asking someone for a direct way of contacting Chuck. The answer was a repeated "No."

"I usually saw Chuck at the bigger shows and auctions, so I just planned on trying to bump into him at Pebble Beach," Kevin says. "I was on the green at Pebble Beach, looking at some magnificent cars on Sunday morning when, out of the corner of my eye, I saw Chuck!" After walking over to him and casually asking how he'd been, Kevin asked, "Remember you told me you were looking for a car that came out of your father's dealership? Was your dad's dealership Spielman Motor Car Company in Brooklyn?"

Chuck confirmed that it was.

"You're not going to believe this," Kevin began, "but there's a black-on-black 1965 fuel injection tanker that might be available."

Kevin recalls Chuck's reaction: "You've got to be kidding me! Kevin, get me the car. I've been looking for 40 years for a car out of my dad's dealership."

The only problem that remained was whether or not the tanker was still for sale, as it had been several months since Kevin had last talked to the dealer who had it in his possession. Chuck had been having problems with his phone system when Kevin tried calling originally and had never received the voice mail. Knowing that the dealer had begun actively promoting the car for sale, Kevin told Chuck that he would have to find out if it was still available. After giving him his new cell phone number, Chuck said, "Kevin, if that car is what it they

Before handing over the keys to Chuck Spielman, Kevin had made a set of license plate tags for Spielman Chevrolet. That was the icing on the cake for Chuck, having the car just the way it sat in his father's dealership, where he happened to work in 1965.

say it is, I want it. Maybe I'd even remember it as a kid; I worked at the dealership in 1965. Don't lose that car!"

The following week, at Corvettes at Carlisle in Pennsylvania, Kevin ran into David, the dealer, and asked about the black Tanker. David responded that someone was coming to the dealership in five days to put down a deposit on it. Kevin's heart sank, but he asked specifically, "Is it sold yet?" David responded that nothing is sold until he gets cash in hand, and that he was asking $325,000 for it.

Kevin immediately called Chuck, who enthusiastically agreed to pay the $325,000 for the ultra-rare car by saying simply, "I'll take it." Being well respected in the business has its perks; David told Kevin that no immediate deposit would be required. The car was as good as Chuck's.

With Chuck's Tanker safely at Corvette Repair, Kevin's team went through it to make it mechanically reliable and safe. The previous owner had done a body-off restoration, which had earned an NCRS Top Flight award, but a couple of things needed to be corrected.

"We made sure that the car was roadworthy because Chuck likes to drive his cars," Kevin says. "We also started the process of hunting down the original owner of the car. Somebody special ordered that car, and there's got to be a cool story. At the end, before shipping it back, we put some Spielman Motor Sales license plates on it for him. Chuck was almost in tears when he saw the car for the first time. He was shaking."

Corvette Repair shipped the car out to California, where it currently rests on a rotisserie in memory of Chuck's father and Spielman Motor Sales. "It's the crown jewel of his collection," Kevin says. "He's got a lot of nice cars, but with his daughter and his grandkids there, this one is very sentimental."

CHAPTER 15

1956 Sebring Racer #3

TRUE PRIVATEERING

The 1956 running of the 12 Hours of Sebring proved to be one of the most important international races in history. At the time, everyone knew it, too. Just six months earlier, Mercedes-Benz driver Pierre Levegh had crashed, flying into the stands full of spectators killing 83 and seriously injuring another 63. Governments were feared to come down hard on racing in the coming years and all the major auto manufacturers and sanctioning bodies took it upon themselves to go into lockdown mode until the future of racing could be decided.

This voluntary pullback couldn't have come at a worse time for the budding Corvette brand. In its first two years, it was seen as a cute and underpowered car that lacked both sports car performance features and luxury appointments, making it somewhat of a nothing car. When Ford's Thunderbird came out in late 1954 with a complete array of luxury power features, powertrain packages, and styling options, Zora Arkus-Duntov knew he needed to take the Corvette to the next level, and fast.

Even with the addition of a 265-ci V-8, Corvette was dominated by Thunderbird in 1955, selling 700 examples that year compared to the Blue Oval model's 16,000. A speed record set at the "Flying Mile" during Daytona Speed Week in 1955 by a specially tuned Corvette made major headway in public perception, but GM brass knew that the best place to prove this fiberglass car's mettle was at Sebring. A strong showing against the best international competition at America's most important racetrack would show Corvette as a true enthusiast sports car. A poor showing would almost certainly doom the Chevrolet brand. The fate of the Corvette rested on those 12 hours in March.

Although it's likely that no one wanted to see Corvette succeed more than Zora Arkus-Duntov, he was against running a factory-backed team with so little prep time and especially after the Le Mans accident. He didn't think the Corvette brakes were up to the challenge, and he wanted more time for testing and engineering. After voicing his concerns, he was replaced by driver John Fitch, who later headed the Corvette racing program under Chevrolet General Manager Ed Cole.

While Fitch went to Florida to put a team and cars together, Arkus-Duntov remained in Detroit engineering and re-engineering parts. When each part was finished, he added it to the Chevrolet parts catalog to maintain homologation standards. By the time everything

The only private-entry Corvette to run at Sebring in 1956 was the #3 car owned by Carl Beuhler, who drove it from Chicago to Sebring, Florida, for the campaign. He retained the Arctic Blue paint scheme, which matches beautifully with the red interior and differentiated it from the professional entries that were white with blue racing stripes. (Photo Courtesy Kevin Mackay Collection)

was in place, the Corvette racing operation had only five weeks to build tough cars capable of not only surviving Sebring, but winning. The race cars were developed using 1955 chassis, but because they were running in 1956, they were fitted with special 1956 prototype bodies to show off the Corvette's new look to the public. The one exception was the #7 car, which used an early 1956 chassis.

Under the guise of Raceway Enterprises, Chevrolet ran four factory Corvettes at Sebring that year, #1, #5, #6, and #7. The first car, known to Corvette enthusiasts as "The Real McCoy," was the same prototype that had set the speed record at Daytona. It wore #1 due to its starting position, which it earned by having the largest engine, a 307-ci V-8 that was mated to a ZF 4-speed and placed it in the B production class. The other "factory" cars retained their 265-ci 3-speed powertrains and raced in the C production class. Two of the 265-powered factory racers were forced to drop out within the first hour. That year proved to be difficult for all teams involved, as it saw only 24 of the original 60 starters cross the finish line after 12 hours.

The #1 prototype car, wearing #1, driven by John Fitch and Walt Hansgen, was one such car to roar across the finish line, finishing 1st in its class and 9th overall. The second factory Corvette finished not too far behind in 15th place overall and 7th in its more challenging class, having gone up against the venerable factory Ferraris and Jaguars.

Chevrolet trumpeted the #1 car in print ads all over the place after the class win, and Corvette became an instant sensation in the world of international racing and in dealership showrooms. Sales jumped to 3,467 cars in 1956 and 6,339 in 1957. Sales continued to climb from there following success after success.

The #3 Corvette

Somewhat lost in the shuffle of the high-profile factory race team entrants was a privateer racer that placed 23rd overall, a remarkable feat considering that nearly two-thirds of the field failed to finish. The #3 Corvette had possibly a longer journey to Sebring than the factory cars did.

Carl C. Beuhler III was a successful businessman and aspiring racer in addition to being a great customer and friend of Dick Doane Chevrolet outside Chicago. Doane Chevrolet was a popular performance shop often used by General Motors to build race cars that it couldn't technically build in-house. The factory Sebring racers were no exception, and they saw their initial shipment and setup there.

In the dealership's service area one day, Beuhler saw these special cars with 1955 frames and 1956 bodies being worked on. He spoke to his friend Dick Doane about ordering one for himself to campaign at Sebring that year. Doane was successful in his attempt to secure a fifth car from Chevrolet for his customer to enter on his own.

Unlike the factory entries, which sported the standard American white and blue stripe paint scheme used in international racing, Beuhler ordered his in stunning Arctic Blue with a red interior. Also unlike the factory racers, when his car was ready just before Sebring, Beuhler picked it up at Doane Chevrolet in Chicago and drove it the 1,200-plus miles to Sebring just in time for the race. Before the competition, all five Corvettes were parked together for a picture. The factory team cars lined up perfectly facing the camera; Beuhler pulled his car in straight and off to the side, facing away from the camera. After surviving the race that saw so many competitors forced to drop out, Beuhler loaded his Corvette and drove it back to Chicago.

While being serviced back at Dick Doane Chevrolet after the race, one of the 4-barrel Carter carburetors caught fire and engulfed the car, causing severe body damage. Beuhler didn't want the car after that, and he traded it in on a 300SL. Doane Chevrolet rebodied the car correctly as a 1955 Corvette and sold it. And although there were only 700 1955 Corvettes ever made, this one fell into place alongside all the others.

[illegible]
4330-F DR M B KENLAY,545 SHERIDAN RD,WINNETKA-DOD [illegible] ED4454932
4331-J M DRENNAN,[illegible] CARMEN AV-CHEV [illegible] EHAD264825
[illegible] KAUFMANN,[illegible] LAKEVIEW AV-OLDS [illegible] ER521388
[illegible] ARMITAGE AV-MERC [illegible]
4334-MRS [illegible] SERIO,146 N LATROBE AV-MERC [illegible]
4335-V ANDERSON,5923 N PAULINA ST-CHEV FC53F055088 ELAQ224424
4336-G R BARROW,706 E 13TH,GIBSON CITY-CHEV F3AH1220175 EAA343377
4337-V DONARSKI,2124 S GUNDERSON,BERWYN-PON FP755H115446
4338-H A GOODWIN,7454 N HOYNE AV-CAD E526243341
4339-G A CONNER,428 NORMAL PKWY-BU [illegible]
4340-S KELLERMANN,JR,203 S BENTON,EDWARDSVILLE-BU F45660370 E58990565
4341-J F W PEACOCK,[illegible] W HUBBARD ST-LIN [illegible]
4342-A J CLAVIN,1012 LOCUST,STERLING-CHEV FB55J091312 [illegible]
4343-M E GRIFFIN,713 VOGEL PL,E ST LOUIS-FORD [illegible]
[illegible] N RICHMOND ST-FORD [illegible]
4345-D M WALTERS,GREEN TOP FARM,[illegible]-MERC [illegible]
4346-C BUEHLER,[illegible] PALATINE-[illegible]
4347-M M SCHAFER,[illegible] N LOCKWOOD AV-OLDS [illegible]
4348-J A SANDERS,854 W OAKDALE AV-CHEV F21HKH66623 EHAA901673
4349-C L MCGINN,BOX 48 RIVER RD,STERLING-STUD F4369749 EH337021
4350-R S THARP,1300 N 5TH,SPRINGFIELD-OLDS F508M50901 E8A377843H
4351-B J KRAL,4338 W NORTH AV-CAD [illegible]
4352-H W WING,1117 ASBURY AV,EVANSTON-CHEV FB53J045072 ELAQ188958
4353-M E KLEIN,40 E OAK ST-PON FP8ZH47303
4354-J B CRISSEY,818 N ELMWOOD,OAK PK-BU F5B1095697 EV10072185
4355-O L BETTAG,MD,6500 W IRVING PARK RD-CAD F516299573
4356-THE STEARNES CO,1333 S WABASH AV-CAD E546019466
4357-E M MOWEN,[illegible] S RACINE AV-CHRY F7094384 EC461604
4358-C F KERBS,3825 W BYRON-FORD EA3PG163992
4359-J STICKELS,327 PARK,CLARENDON HILLS-FORD EB300164017

After coming across a picture showing the car's license plate, C1 expert Loren Lundberg wrote to the Illinois Department of Motor Vehicles and received this microfiche copy in return. It's difficult to make out, but Carl Beuhler (misspelled) III is listed alongside the Corvette's serial number along with his address and telephone number. Modern privacy laws would likely prevent anyone from obtaining this information today.

In 1985, noted C1 expert Loren Lundberg was looking through old racing photos when he happened across that shot of the five Corvettes that ran at Sebring in 1956. The four white and blue cars are immediately recognizable as factory racers, but the Arctic Blue #3 car was obviously a private entry. Loren was amazed at the clarity and definition of the photo and, after studying it, something interesting popped out at him that you don't usually see on race cars. Because the #3 car was pulled in haphazardly, he could easily make out the Illinois license plate number: 4346.

In 1985, it required only a simple phone call to the Illinois Department of Motor Vehicles to obtain microfiche data records containing the car's VIN number and the owner's name and address. The VIN number came up as #24, making Beuhler's Corvette the 24th car produced in 1955.

Lundberg told Kevin about his discovery to gauge his thoughts on the entire story. Kevin told him that it would be an amazing car to go after, so Lundberg continued with his search, tracing the VIN to the current owner in Florida, who turned out to be a professional golfer. He had had the car expertly restored and had won a Bloomington Gold, NCRS Top Flight, and Arkus-Duntov Award, with everyone under the impression that the car's fame derived from its super-early production date.

The golfer wanted $100,000, not an unreasonable amount for the car around the year 2000 when Kevin first tried to secure it. But in as-raced condition it would only be worth between $200,000 to $250,000. Race car values just hadn't skyrocketed yet; Kevin had recently sold *the Rebel* car for only $350,000. Compared to the other cars Kevin was finding and spending time on, it just didn't make much sense to tie up that kind of money.

"I would have been too buried in the car," Kevin points out the quagmire of running a business and following his passion. "So I kept an eye on it, but after a while I forget about it."

One of Kevin's longtime customers, Phil Schwartz, was starting to develop an impressive collection of Corvettes at his home on Long Island. He could often be found at Corvette Repair on Saturdays, learning from Kevin and talking about future purchases and what was going on in the hobby. Every now and then they discussed the 1956 #3 Sebring car and Schwartz took a liking to it. It would make a great car to add to his collection, and after hearing about some of Kevin's famous L88 buys, he thought they might be able to "steal" it. This

Corvette Repair customer Phil Schwartz purchased the Sebring Corvette, which had been restored to supposedly correct 1955 spec by a previous owner, since the car's serial numbers all said 1955. Luckily, the restoration left many of the prototype 1956 components still on the car. Kevin sourced a 1956 body to use to bring the car to its correct, original racing prototype livery.

was around 2010, and the value of a Sebring racer with an interesting history had grown to well over $250,000!

Kevin's first move was to call the golfer to find out if he still had it. He didn't, but he had sold it to a dealer in Georgia. The dealership's website showed the '55 Corvette with VIN #24 as having been sold. A phone call to the dealer revealed that the car was sold to a customer in Texas.

"I have a customer who has a great interest in that car," Kevin told the dealer representative. "Of course I wasn't going to bring up the words race car, Sebring, or #3; that never crossed my mind. We were trying to get the car and if they knew what it was, they probably wouldn't sell it."

He was told that the car definitely wasn't for sale, but if they were willing to pay $185,000, something could potentially be worked out. "The best '55 on the planet would take only $150,000," Kevin told the dealer, incredulous at the asking price.

"Well, see, the car's not for sale," the dealer reminded him. "So if you really want this car you're going to have to pay crazy money for it."

Schwartz didn't want anything to do with it. "That's ridiculous!" he said, having hoped to pay a discounted price on a car that would need a complete nut-and-bolt rebuild to bring it back to Sebring spec.

"Phil, the car's a million-dollar car; what the hell's $185,000?" Kevin told him.

"Okay, get the damn car," Schwartz replied.

Kevin took the dealer up on his offer, and the car was shipped directly to Corvette Repair. The '55 was restored beautifully by the previous shop. Luckily, the car still had a lot of forensic evidence that pointed to its racing heritage. The floor, which had originally housed a 3-speed manual shifter had been fabricated to accept a correct-for-1955 Powerglide automatic shifter.

As part of the restoration, Schwartz bought a '56 Corvette to use for its original body and panels while Corvette Repair returned the floor to its 3-speed configuration. The 265 engine had been replaced with a single-carburetor one that was date-coded to 1955 in addition to a proper Powerglide. The 3-speed manual didn't come out until

It took two years to complete the restoration of the #3 Sebring racer back to its 1956 prototype livery. Due to the car's historical significance and exacting restoration, it was awarded an NCRS American Heritage Award. Notice the tiny windscreen and the leather hood safety latches. Do you think Carl Beuhler drove all the way from Chicago to Sebring in March with that little thing?

It's not often you see a side-dump exhaust on a C1, and it sure looks good on this Arctic Blue thriller. One can only imagine the beautiful sounds that emanate from it.

late 1955 and wouldn't have been available on a car with such an early VIN. Corvette Repair had to source a rare dual-carb manifold with an early 1956 date code and a pair of Carter 4-barrels. A correct tachometer and racing driving lights also had to be found. The restoration took two years to complete and was awarded an NCRS American Heritage Award in 2014.

"This is all because Loren found a photograph with the license plate on it and happened to run it when you were allowed to run that stuff without getting someone in trouble. It's one of five cars that went to Sebring in 1956 and the only private entry car. It's just a striking car in what is essentially red, white, and blue, which is cool. It's now part of the Phil Schwartz collection and he shows it all over the place. People love it. It's a well-documented, amazing car."

In 2017 Phil Schwartz celebrated his 70th birthday in style, with the centerpiece being a $5,000 custom birthday cake modeled after the Arctic Blue #3 car.

CHAPTER 16

1966 8-Ball Racer

THE START OF DOUG BERGEN'S AND BOB JOHNSON'S CAREERS

Businessman Doug Bergen of Marietta, Ohio, loved driving his 1963 Corvette so much that he decided that he wanted to try his hand at local SCCA racing. The year was 1966, and like most aspiring racers without a factory connection, he went to his local dealership, Williston Chevrolet, and purchased a 1966 427/425 big-block coupe with all the available race-prep options, including an M21 4-speed transmission and radio delete. He ordered it in his favorite color combination of Tuxedo Black over Saddle interior.

When his new race car arrived, he modified it as any racer would. He added a single hood pin and roll bar for safety, pulled the bumpers for weight savings, and popped in a racing seat on the driver's side. He also opened up the side vents on the 1966 big-block hood and added a pair of mirrors to the fenders. He ran the car himself in local autocross races, oftentimes competing against his friend Bob Johnson, who drove a Sunbeam Tiger.

Bob Johnson had developed a reputation as one of the best drivers in the area, and when Bergen's Corvette was invited to compete at the national race at Cumberland Airport in May 1966, he was asked to drive. Expertly piloting the powerful Corvette, Johnson took a first-place finish in that race. He also took first in the Johnny Appleseed 150 at Mid-Ohio in August, and at Marlboro, Maryland, in September. The stage was set for a fruitful partnership between Bergen and Johnson, the Marietta men, and Bergen asked Johnson if he would drive the car for the 1967 season. Except this time, they would compete in the SCCA's A Production class against even better national competitors.

The Bergen/Johnson team, which now also included Bill "Murph" Mayberry spinning wrenches, was poised for success in 1967. Murph's connections with Roger Penske and Chevrolet allowed him to secure many of the secret race parts that the other top teams were receiving from Development and Engineering. With continued strong finishes in 1967, Bergen became a regular face in the pits and soon befriended Don Yenko. Yenko filled him in on the L88 program being worked on at Chevrolet and told him that parts were available to bring a regular 427 up to L88 spec. Soon after, Bergen's engine developed internal damage that would require a complete teardown and rebuild. His first call was to Don Yenko, who rebuilt the engine as an L88.

Bergen and Johnson competed during the rest of the 1967 season with the L88 engine, seeing enough success to be invited to the

Doug Bergen (left) and Bob Johnson (right) stand beside the restored 1966 8-Ball racer at the National Corvette Museum. This was Bergen's first racing effort, which was successfully taken to the national level with Johnson at the helm. You can just make out the side vents on the hood cowl that Bergen enlarged in order to get more cool air into the air filter. (Jerry Heasley Photo)

Daytona Runoffs, although a blown head gasket forced the team to a 7th-place finish. The car ran in its regular black and yellow paint scheme, but the number 8 on the side, written in a white circle against the black paint earned it the nickname "8-Ball." After the 1967 season, Bergen had developed enough pull with Chevrolet to receive one of 80 1968 L88s for the next year. He converted the '66 back to stock configuration, which included pulling the L88 engine and replacing it.

Behind the 8-Ball

Doug Bergen and Bob Johnson went on to field the '68 L88 for two seasons before upgrading to a '69 L88, which unfortunately wasn't ready until the 1970 season. The '69 was only raced for one season before Bergen sold it to VV Cooke.

In his hunt for winning L88 race cars, Kevin hunted down and purchased the VV Cooke car. In doing research on that car, he discovered that Doug Bergen and Bob Johnson had raced other successful Corvettes together, including a '66 that ran at the Daytona Runoffs as an L88. After contacting Doug Bergen and developing a friendship with him, Kevin was given the car's VIN number, which he had tracked down by his investigator, David Reisner.

The Corvette was traced to just 100 miles away from Bergen's home in Marietta, Ohio, and was owned by a guy in the landscaping business. He had purchased it from the second owner in 1975 and painted it in what Kevin describes as "Lawn Green." Sure enough, the VIN matched, and the car still sported its original saddle interior.

The kicker for Kevin was that one of the car's owners had put a custom plate with a radio in it where the original radio would have gone. It must have originally been a radio-delete car. Kevin could also see evidence that hood pins had once been installed. He bought the car for $35,000 before selling it to his customer, Marc Mehl, who promised that Corvette Repair would get the complete restoration.

A transport truck picked up the Corvette and took it to Corvette Repair for further pre-restoration analysis. Doug Bergen was even flown in to certify the car as having originally been his first race car. Although the numbers matched, a confirmation from the original owner is an important piece of the puzzle when it comes to race cars that have been abused and had parts swapped in and out over the years. This one, like many others, had been converted back to street trim, with very few clues as to its racing heritage, much less that it was the actual *8-Ball* racer.

Doug Bergen walked around the car, inspecting every detail as he went. He remained silent. It had been many years since he had last seen the '66 Corvette, and the green street car in front of him bore no resemblance to it at all.

"I'm really sorry, Kevin, but I can't remember anything on this car," he said finally.

Kevin understood why Bergen couldn't recognize anything, but it wasn't good to hear him say it aloud. He pointed to the holes in the fenders where his mirrors would have been mounted. "Yeah, I see the holes, but I can't confirm it as of yet."

Then Bergen remembered something. A tiny detail from nearly 30 years before that only he knew about. If it was there, then the car was without a doubt his old race car. He walked around to the driver's side and opened the door. He lifted up the driver-side carpet and the accelerator pedal, then peered underneath. "Son of a gun!" he exclaimed. "I can't believe it's still there!"

Everyone following along at Corvette Repair stepped closer to the driver-side door in curiosity, asking, "Doug, what is it!?"

Bergen pointed to a little piece of aluminum diamond plate, a 2 x 4–inch rectangle positioned underneath the pedal. "I made that plate and put it in the car," he said. "The gas pedal was cracking the fiberglass from being pressed so hard and I wanted to give it some support. So I made that little metal thing in my warehouse. I made it myself, I drilled the holes in it, and I put it in the car. This is absolutely my car!"

Kevin and his team were overjoyed, as was Bergen who leapt up and jumped around the car in excitement. He congratulated Mehl on being the owner of his first race car before hugging Kevin. The green '66 was officially confirmed as the car that kicked off the successful racing careers of Doug Bergen and "Marietta" Bob Johnson.

After he confirmed the *8-Ball* car, Kevin took Bergen to his house to see the VV Cooke car. He recognized his own handiwork immediately on the fuel cell, which his manufacturing company had made and he had personally installed in the car.

Corvette Repair then initiated a complete restoration of the car back to its 1967 Daytona Runoffs trim, which included both Bergen's and Johnson's names on the quarter panel. In the original photos of the car, there's a decal that Kevin couldn't make out, so he asked Bergen if he possibly remembered it. Not only did he remember it (it happened to be the logo for Bob Johnson's business), but still had one at his house. Kevin had the original decal scanned and duplicated and put the new one on the car.

"That car's Daytona Runoffs trim is probably one of the prettiest cars I've ever seen," Kevin says. "Black with the big 8-ball on the side and the yellow stripe, it's just a gorgeous car."

Following the restoration, Bergen and Johnson were reunited with the car at the National Corvette Museum. It was just as they'd remembered it from 1967.

No, the antenna wasn't glassed over; this is a real radio-delete race car. Doug Bergen originally ordered the car in black with a tan interior and once it was in his shop he added all the race goodies like roll bar, fender-mounted mirrors, and race wheels. The number eight inset in a white circle against the black car makes it easy to see where its nickname came from. (Jerry Heasley Photo)

Doug Bergen (left) and Bob Johnson leaning up against the 8-Ball racer at the 1967 SCCA runoffs at Daytona. The L88 upgrade on the Corvette had been completed and the car competed in the runoffs in that trim. Johnson had only been racing professionally for three months by this time. (Photo Courtesy Kevin Mackay Collection)

CHAPTER 17

1965 Mark IV Heavy-Duty Test Engine

THE MOTOR THAT WOULD BECOME THE L88

While the Grand Sport Corvettes continued to compete out on the racetracks, Zora Arkus-Duntov and his team, which included right-hand man Gib Hufstader, continued developing an engine package that they knew would be the future for competition Corvettes.

The big-block engine program was initially called Mark II, which led to the creation of the 396-ci big-block and followed quickly by the 427-ci big-block. But the effort to harness those large-displacement powerplants into racing engines was dubbed Mark IV, which went on to be known as Regular Production Option (RPO) L88.

Arkus-Duntov's team took one of the 396 test engines and bored it to 427 ci in addition to enhancing the fuel flow with worked heads, a single 4-barrel carburetor, and prototype headers. The engine was ready for the ultimate test just in time for the 1965 12 Hours of Sebring, but with Chevrolet having no official involvement in racing, Arkus-Duntov needed a creative way to get his engine into a privately owned Grand Sport.

He decided it should go to the first Grand Sport coupe, Grand Sport #003, which was owned by 19-year-old Alan Sevadjian of Arlington, Texas. All five Grand Sports were still in heavy competition at the time and remained competitive into the early 1970s. Arkus-Duntov called Delmo Johnson of Johnson Chevrolet in Dallas, Texas, one of the drivers of the car who would be joined by Ed Sevadjian, Alan's father, and Dave Morgan at Sebring, and told him he had a special engine for him to run in the Grand Sport coupe.

Because mailing an engine out of the Engineering and Development shop at General Motors would have raised some eyebrows, Arkus-Duntov managed to smuggle it to the Corvette assembly plant in St. Louis. There, it was installed in a white 1965 convertible destined for Johnson Chevrolet.

Carrying the special Mark IV engine safely between its fender wells, it rode along with the other Chevrolets until it reached its final destination. Johnson's team was under strict instructions from Arkus-Duntov not to touch anything on the engine and to simply remove it from the convertible and place it into the Grand Sport coupe. Johnson admitted years later that they ended up dropping the oil pan from the engine against Arkus-Duntov's wishes. And they're lucky they did. A disgruntled union worker at the St. Louis plant had dropped some cotter pins into the crankcase, which would have likely caused catastrophic damage on the first practice lap.

This shot by Dave Nicholas perfectly sums up the 1965 running of the 12 Hours of Sebring. Kevin's Duntov-built Mark IV motor powered Grand Sport 003 (wearing #1 here) around the wet Florida track that day. (Photo Courtesy BarcBoys.com)

Damage did occur on the practice laps for the team, as Johnson crashed the car. Although it was able to be repaired for the race, they were hardly capable of competing against the other teams that were better staffed, better prepared, and had more backup parts. The weather that year was horrendous as well, with hurricane-like conditions making it nearly impossible to see. Water stood more than a foot deep on some parts of the Central Florida track. But the #003 Grand Sport Corvette (featuring #1 on the doors) and its prototype Mark IV engine was fast. It screamed down the straightaway at 180 mph and threatened to break loose with each press of the accelerator. It was essentially a drag car, and it struggled with the turns. The car was so powerful that the front lifted enough on acceleration to make the wheels leave the ground and the steering next to impossible.

Even with everything going on around it, the #1 team managed to finish the race, albeit in 36th place. For them, it was a disaster. For Arkus-Duntov's vision of a durable and powerful racing engine, it was a success.

The mule car was always thought to have been meant to originally receive a big-block engine, but after discovering the car not too long ago, Kevin found it to be a small-block 365-hp car and not a big-block.

For those curious about whatever happened to the white convertible delivery car that technically was the first recipient of the Mark IV engine, that car has been located and the family who owns it is currently enjoying it and has no interest in selling.

See-Through Corvette Number Two

When Kevin Mackay was handed the engine by his customer at the time, Victor Preisler, it was covered in special experimental prototype serial numbers and came with all the engineering work orders to prove that it was indeed the first Mark IV service package engine.

With just the engine sitting at Corvette Repair, Kevin knew it would make for another great addition to his long line of unique creations. He decided to build a see-through 1965 Corvette coupe complete with all the special, heavy-duty, service package items that would come with a car meant for racing. The build includes a 36-gallon tank, a "Tanker," along with big brakes, an M22 transmission, and heavy-duty shocks and springs. Like the '69 see-through car that came before it, this one was given the complete treatment

This see-through 1965 Corvette made the perfect show mule for Kevin's 1965 Mark IV Heavy Duty test motor. Everything on it is completely functional, correct, and street legal! (Photo Courtesy Bill Erdman)

in terms of floating emblems, functional lights, horn, wipers, and anything else to make it street legal. While it was at Kevin's shop, Preisler's interests changed, and he sold the engine to another of Kevin's customers, Ed Foss, who continued with the special project.

One of the most special parts on the car is a clear valve cover given to Kevin by Mike Yager of Mid America Motorworks. He had some of them made for his engine displays, and it fits right in with the car. Not only does the engine run with the special valve cover, you can see the rocker arms moving back and forth underneath as they're lubricated. You can literally see Zora Arkus-Duntov's development heads at work.

The car is entirely street legal, but remember, it's the same engine that propelled Grand Sport #003 to 180 mph at Sebring in 1965 and that its drivers struggled to keep it under control.

"The engine is so powerful that if you put the gas pedal down to the floor, you'll kill yourself," Kevin points out. "It's so light it's dangerous. I tried to put the pedal down one time and I was afraid to. You just spin the wheels and the thing takes off like a rocket ship, like a slingshot. It's ridiculous. And you've got that driveshaft spinning right there. If you hit it too hard, that driveshaft may snap and hit you in the leg. It's inches away. And what you really don't want to do is hold it or lean on it by mistake, or get a belt or piece of clothing wrapped up in it. Now I drive it like an old lady."

The thing that Kevin is most proud of when it comes to his driveable see-through creations is that they give people an opportunity to see all the engineering Chevrolet did to make the car work. You can see how close the driveshaft actually is to your hip and leg; it's usually covered by a carpeted and covered tunnel. You can see the gas tank right behind the seats and even watch the windows go up and down. The windows are the same on every Corvette, so anyone who owns a mid-year can watch their car at work.

"Everything is just so exposed," Kevin says. "It's the inner workings of a Corvette. If someone is in the middle of a restoration and doesn't know where something goes, it provides the perfect map. You don't even need a flashlight or have to crawl under the car to see anything. It takes a tremendous amount of research and there were hours spent making every tiny detail perfect. Components such as cotter pins, screws, washers, bolts, and brackets are all different colors. There are hundreds of thousands of little parts that we have to get right, and that's what makes these cars so special."

CHAPTER 18

1971 Sideways ZR2

THE BADDEST BIG-BLOCK

By 1970, the storied 427 big-block had been replaced by the modern muscle car era 454 big-block. Just as the 427 had been offered in a track-ready L88 performance trim, the 454 was available in the Chevelle with an underrated 450-hp LS6 engine. However, it wasn't until 1971 that this engine was available in the Corvette and a true successor to the L88 came to market. Of the 188 Corvettes that were ordered with the LS6 engine in 1971, 12 were equipped with the special ZR2 Off Road Package.

The ZR2

The ZR2 Corvette was Chief Engineer Zora Arkus-Duntov's final high-performance factory special, and many consider it to be his greatest triumph. At the very least, it's definitely one of the rarest big-blocks, with 1971 being the only year of production. At the heart of the ZR2 is the 454 LS6 with aluminum heads; forged crank, rods, and pistons; heavy-duty four-bolt main; and solid lifters backed by a heavy-duty close-ratio M22 4-speed Rock Crusher transmission. A transistorized ignition and high-capacity aluminum radiator were also included, just as on the previous L88. F41 heavy-duty suspension, J56 heavy-duty power brakes, 4:11 rear axle with Posi-Traction, and radio-delete were all part of the track package.

The Sideways Corvette

In 2010, Kevin Mackay and the Corvette Repair team began the restoration of one of the 12 ZR2s, VIN 194371S118181, owned by Ed Foss, who, at the time, owned the largest collection of 1970–1972 ZR cars in the world. The car is one of two Canadian-export ZR2s, this one having been delivered to Golden Mile Chev Olds in Toronto and sold to original owner Barry Needler.

During the restoration, Kevin found himself at the Barrett-Jackson auction looking at the generous display of brand-new Mustangs that Ford was showing off. One of them was on its side, looking as if it would come tumbling down at any minute. Kevin walked up to the display and instead of looking at the hot new Mustang, he admired the display rig that allowed the car to safely be shown in that position. The black metal rig was a mechanical work of art that used a series of wheels and leverage bars to raise the car on its side and then bring it

What makes a 1971 ZR2 Corvette stand out from your run-of-the-mill 454 big-block is usually hidden from sight. A powerful, race-prepped engine mixed with heavy-duty transmission, gearing, brakes, and suspension all combine to make the ZR2 the pinnacle of the pre-emissions Corvettes. To the casual observer, they're all hidden underneath the body.

back down again to be transported. He instantly knew that the next Corvette Repair Unique Creation had to be a sideways Corvette.

When Kevin got home, he browsed the Internet to find the manufacturer of the sideways car display that he had seen at Ford. He had taken nearly 100 pictures of the contraption and recognized it as soon as he saw it online. He was able to buy one through the website for $1,800 and eagerly awaited its arrival.

Kevin knew just the car to attach to his new sideways rig. Few people had seen a ZR2 Corvette, but from the outside, like most special Corvettes, it really didn't look all that special. The real magic of the ZR2 Corvette lay in its powertrain package and suspension. Combined with the fact that most people never saw that on even a base-model Corvette, Kevin wanted to show the car as a chassis and powertrain.

Ed Foss's ZR2 was the perfect example to display. All the GM paperwork was with the car, and the team debuted it at the NCRS National Convention in Michigan in 2011. Crowds went nuts over the beauty of the detailed chassis shown suspended for easy, up-close

Once its show tour was completed as a sideways display Corvette, Kevin took the ZR2 chassis off the rig to finish the restoration. The end result is this stunning green/green coupe. (Photo Courtesy Bill Erdman)

viewing. They showed the display at Bloomington and Corvettes at Carlisle afterward and it became another instant marketing hit for the business.

Following its use as the famous Sideways Corvette, this particular ZR2 was completed in its original Brands Hatch Green with Dark Green vinyl interior. It once again saw public attention when it was auctioned off at the 2014 Barrett-Jackson Scottsdale auction, selling for $495,000.

CHAPTER 19

1957 Airbox Corvette

THE RETRIEVAL OPERATION

The success that Corvette had at Sebring in 1956 led to an about-face for the ailing little sports car. It took on the feel and performance associated with European exotics in 1956, but 1957 is when Corvette truly became America's Sports Car and could compete with the best. After Carl Beuhler's finish as a privateer at Sebring, even more Corvettes were available to amateurs in 1957. Seven different engine options, all based on the uprated 283-ci engine, became available backed by three transmission options, three differential options, and a special racing suspension package. If you wanted to go racing in 1957, your local Chevy dealer was about as far as you needed to look to make that happen.

The hallmark of Corvette's high-performance engine options was the all-new Rochester mechanical fuel injection, with owners calling the cars "Fuelies" for short. The drivetrain packages could be designed to suit any use, including just having something fast for the street. The highest-performing carburetor option, RPO 469C, included a pair of 4-barrels that put out 270 hp with a 9.5:1 compression ratio. Of the 6,339 Corvette customers, more than half chose one of the two dual-carb packages.

In terms of fuel-injected cars, there were several options. If you were one of the 284 customers who wanted to run a Powerglide automatic with your Fuelie, you'd wind up with 250 hp from a 9.5:1 compression ratio. Most performance buyers, 713 to be exact, went with RPO 579B, which was the same price but was backed by either the stock 3-speed manual or RPO 685 4-speed manual, which was new for 1957. This would be fine for street racing and short, local track races, but the Rochester unit, just like modern fuel injection, hated heat. When General Motors developed the Fuelie engines, engineers set the air intake inside the engine bay to avoid reworking the entire front end.

Extended, high-throttle use could prove to be problematic for the injection unit, but at the very least, it would rob the car of valuable horsepower as it continued to heat up. GM engineers solved this problem, or at least fixed it for the time being, with RPO 579E, which used the same 10.5:1 compression ratio as the B option but cost an additional $242.10 and gained 10 ft-lbs of torque in the process. The option included an 8,000-rpm tachometer mounted front and center on the steering column. The 43 enthusiasts who ordered this package also opted for the 4-speed transmission and $780.10 heavy-duty suspension package.

RPO 579E added a large, handlaid fiberglass tunnel to the driver-side inner fender and a hole in the radiator mount. A tube ran from the hole in the radiator mount, through the fender, and into the air-intake box on the fuel injection unit. Cool, fresh air from the front of the car was essentially delivered directly to the fuel injection unit. Although both fuel injection options were rated with the same 283 hp, under extended use at and above normal engine operating

The Airbox Corvette as it arrived at Corvette Repair for a full restoration job. No one ever said it was easy to put these cars back together again.

temperature, the Airbox cars could provide continuous high performance all day long. A *Road & Track* test done at the time found the Airbox Corvette to run 0–60 in 5.7 seconds.

Of the 43 originally built, only about 18 are believed to still exist. A 1957 Airbox Corvette could easily be the centerpiece of any car collection, and recent sales included one for $875,000 and one for $1 million.

One such Airbox Corvette wound up under the ownership of noted Ferrari and Corvette collector Phil Bachman in 1992. The car he purchased had been heavily raced but was very original, and it needed a restoration before being added to his pristine collection. The man he bought it from, Jim Purvis, had purchased it directly from the original owner and knew of a restorer in Georgia, Gene Tucker, who could take on the project.

The restoration began as any other, with the body and chassis being taken apart at Tucker's shop and the powertrain and injection unit being sent off to specialists. As time passed, the Airbox project was delayed and pushed around the shop. Over the years, both Phil Bachman and Gene Tucker suffered serious strokes and the cars took a back seat to their health. Their families were obviously more concerned with them than cars as well, and the Airbox was forgotten.

The Lost '57 Airbox Car

Martha Bachman and Phil Jr., PB for short, were going through Phil's records one day to get everything in order once his health had stabilized. His Greenville, Tennessee, collection had continued growing every year and the amount of paperwork was tremendous. PB was going through the file cabinets and noticed a folder labeled "1957 Corvette." Not only was all sorts of documentation inside but it also included a title. He knew of no '57 in his father's collection and asked his mother about it.

She remembered the car instantly. She told him that they had bought that car nearly 20 years earlier and that it was being restored someplace in Georgia. PB hopped on his computer and searched the VIN number and he and Martha were shocked that the restoration shop was attempting to put a mechanic's lien on the car. They freaked out, having no idea what to do, the car had been out of their possession for 19 years. Although the Bachman collection consisted mostly of Ferraris and exotics, they had a good friend whom they knew was heavily involved in both Ferrari and Corvette clubs and might be able to help them get their long-lost car back.

They contacted Rick Race, and he immediately knew where to turn. "There's only one guy I know who will get the job done," he said. "He's out of New York; his name's Kevin Mackay. Let me see if he's willing to do this and help you guys."

"Kevin, I have these lovely people in Greenville, Tennessee, who found themselves in a real pickle," Race said after calling Corvette Repair. "Can you help them?"

After he explained the situation, Kevin was willing to assist the Bachman family in getting their car back. He had known Gene Tucker in the 1980s and was confident that he could help resolve the situation. Kevin flew to Georgia, rented a car, and drove to Tucker's shop. It appeared to be abandoned. He knocked on the door. No answer. He started to walk around the grounds behind the shop where old GMC motor homes were parked side by side in the backyard. Behind them was a massive storage facility and in front of it was a man vacuuming out a limousine.

Kevin told the man that he'd like to speak with Gene Tucker. Unfortunately, that was impossible as Gene had had a stroke years earlier and wasn't doing very well. Kevin asked if he could speak with Tucker's wife, whom he remembered and thought might remember

Not much identifies this stripped 1957 Corvette as a rare Airbox high-performance model. Among the sea of Corvettes and parts Kevin found in the warehouse, the red steering wheel on this car caught his eye. He found the serial number written on the body, and after lifting the hood he found the telltale fiberglass box on the driver-side fender-well. This was the car that he was looking for.

him as well, and was given her phone number.

"I couldn't tell her what I was there for," Kevin says. "If I did, they might just keep the car hidden and under cover. So I called Mrs. Tucker on the phone and told her who I was and that I was friends with her husband many years ago. She remembered me from when I was just starting out. I said that I was just passing through the area and that I knew Gene had a lot of Corvettes in his shop and I was hoping to look around."

Mrs. Tucker said that they would love to have Kevin take a look inside the shop. In fact, since her husband's stroke left him in a wheelchair and he wasn't doing well, they were thinking about selling everything.

"So I went in the shop. It's a huge shop, and there was a lot of cars and everything was in disarray. Everything was apart in different sections of the building. I was looking around and I couldn't find any '57 Corvettes. I knew the serial number of the car and had a copy of the title in my rental car, so I started looking at some of the files in the shop. After a few hours, I couldn't find anything."

Once his search of the primary shop turned up nothing, Kevin went around back to try going inside the large storage building. It was locked. He asked Mrs. Tucker if there were any Corvettes or parts in there and she replied that it was packed with Corvettes, but only her son had the key. He'd be home in a little bit.

"So I went to lunch and when I came back a couple of hours later, there was their son, Robby. He's a big guy, in his 40s, probably 6'2" or 6'3". I looked at him and I felt like a little squirt. I told him I was sorry to hear about his dad and that he did some nice work back in the day."

Robby kindly invited Kevin into the warehouse. Kevin brought a video camera with him and started videoing all the cars in the warehouse; there were between 20 and 25 Corvettes in various stages of restoration. Millions of pieces were piled up around them and Kevin knew that the '57 had to be in there.

"I was taking video of all the cars so he didn't get suspicious. Then, out of the corner of my eye, I saw what appeared to be a '56 or '57 Corvette in raw fiberglass. It was down to the shell. Some repair work was done to the front end, but I saw that they had written something on the driver-side rear quarter panel. It was the car's serial number and I knew right away that was the car. The airbox is still glued in, undisturbed on the inner fender well on the driver's front. Son of a gun, I see the red steering wheel. I know the car's black with a red interior."

With the video camera still rolling, Kevin pointed to the '57 shell and asked what it was.

"Oh that's an Airbox car," Robby told him.

"I know it's an Airbox car," Kevin replied, adding, "It's a neat piece. Whose car is this?"

"We don't know whose car this is; it was abandoned. Some guy had my dad restore it and the guy never called us after that, and he didn't pay his bill. We're going to own this car real soon. We're in the courts right now trying to get a title to the car."

"That's why I'm here. I have the title to the car. It's owned by a lovely couple in Tennessee named Phil and Martha Bachman." Robby turned white. Kevin showed him a copy of the title. "They sent me here to pick up this car. Now I know the car is here. I took pictures of it; I have it on video."

"Well, I don't know whose it is," Robby replied.

"That's funny because we have the receipts. Mr. Bachman was paying the restoration bill and a lot of it is signed by you, Robby, and your mother. I'm not here to have a problem; I'm here to do the right thing. You should give up the car."

Robby informed Kevin that the car had been there for 19 years and that it was their car. Kevin wasn't going to press the issue, but he

Airbox Corvettes earn their name from a special high-performance package that equipped the Rochester fuel injection unit with a fiberglass tunnel on the driver-side fender that brought cold air in from the front of the car. The mechanical fuel injection unit would begin to lose horsepower as it heated up, which made endurance races like Sebring and Daytona difficult. GM engineers fitted a small number of cars with an "airbox," as shown here.

told him that he hoped that they could all work something out, that the Bachmans paid a lot of money for the car and due to similar bad fortunes in both families, they found themselves in this situation.

"The right thing to do is give up the car," Kevin said as his final suggestion.

The response was two words: "Sue me."

"And so Mr. Bachman retained a high-powered attorney and sued the Tuckers. It went on for a little while. You don't know what's going to happen in court. A lot of judges aren't car people. Some have interest in these cases and some have no interest whatsoever. I've found that out firsthand."

The battle continued in court, with Kevin helping the Bachmans in any way he could, but he still shuddered at the idea of a technicality or a misunderstanding costing them the car.

One day he received a call from Martha Bachman. "Kevin, they want to settle. If I pay $75,000 in storage fees, they'll give up the car."

Kevin's advice came quickly: "Settle. Pay 'em. It'll cost you more than that in legal fees if it goes to trial. Pay 'em and get the car out of there."

With the court case settled and Kevin arranging for the car and parts to be picked up and taken to Greenville, he flew to Tennessee to inspect the car and boxes of parts. Some boxes were labeled and others weren't. When everything finally arrived at Corvette Repair, he categorized it all and began the restoration.

Some pieces were missing, such as chrome and other trim pieces, but the car had its original engine, transmission, injection unit, and date-coded shocks. All the valuable and important stuff was there to begin the restoration. Most importantly, the factory airbox unit was still intact.

Well, all the important pieces except one: the VIN tag. To win any major awards, which they hoped to do, you had to declare the VIN tag. "What the hell are we going to do now?" Kevin asked. "The car was a real car, bought from the original owner, and I couldn't believe the VIN tag was missing. At first we thought that it might have been with the other missing parts that we assumed were still at the Tucker's. But there was nothing we could do about it."

To make up for the missing hardware and trim, they purchased an entire donor car, which was easier and cheaper than finding everything bit by bit, and continued the restoration without the VIN tag. After they were a good year or two into the project, Kevin received a text from Martha Bachman. She had been going through some old files and lo and behold, the original VIN tag was right there in an envelope.

While they were working on the Airbox car, Corvette Repair was also freshening up the Bachmans' '67 Tri-Power car that Phil had purchased new and only had 8,000 original miles on it. It was invited to Bloomington to try for a Gold award and a Benchmark award, which is one of the most difficult in the Corvette hobby to achieve. After it won the Benchmark, Phil wanted his '68 big-block done, another car he had purchased new and only put 13,000 miles on, to go for a Benchmark award. It also took one home. Between these projects, Corvette Repair continued to make progress on the '57 Airbox.

In 2016, Kevin gave the Bachmans his word that the car would be done in time for Bloomington 2017, the 60th anniversary of the 1957 Corvette. That would be the time to debut the car that had spent nearly half of its life hidden away.

"So we got the car all done, finished it up. It came out like a piece of jewelry and was a big, big hit. People loved it. They were blown away. People had heard the story, but no one had ever seen the car. When Phil came up to it for the first time (he can barely walk so he's in an electric scooter), all he could say was, 'Oh my god, oh my god, oh my god.' He was stunned when he saw the car and his wife was so happy, too.

"It turned out to be a happy ending even after all the twists and turns of hunting down the car, hunting down the parts, and paying a $75,000 storage fee. The car finally came back to life.

"We just shipped the car two days ago. It's going back to Phil's home because he's having an 80th birthday party, and they invited me down, too. He's been in the car business for 50 years, his car just turned 60, and he just turned 80, so 2017 is a special year for him. And he's one of the nicest people you can ever meet."

After 20-plus years, the Bachmans finally got their 1957 Airbox Corvette back and completely restored. It's easy to see why Kevin refers to this car as "a piece of jewelry." (Photo Courtesy Bill Erdman)

CHAPTER 20

Special Engine Finds

As Kevin Mackay learned early on in his Corvette career, when it comes to the restoration of America's Sports Car, they're all virtually the same, with the primary difference being the powertrain package. Corvette enthusiasts have long referred to cars by their engine option, further highlighting the distinction. A small-block car might be referred to as a 327-300 or a Fuelie. Corvette owners also clarify the difference between a low-horsepower 427 and a 435 Tri-Power. Of course, when it comes to Corvettes, L88 race motors reign supreme in the eyes of most enthusiasts. But in the Corvette universe, there is always a faster, better, rarer Corvette. Oftentimes, Kevin finds one of these faster, better, rarer engines that are worth more by themselves than most whole Corvettes are. When it comes to engines, few are as rare or as valuable as these, and Kevin found himself at the right place at the right time to purchase them.
—Tyler Greenblatt

1967 ZL1 Development Engine

By 1967, Zora Arkus-Duntov's engineering department had mastered the L88 engine package and put it into production with great success on the racetrack. But he knew that his team could make an engine with more horsepower in a lighter package by basing it on an aluminum block instead of a cast-iron one. The new development engine put out 585 hp, 35 more than a standard L88, and it weighed about as much as a 327 small-block.

When Regular Production Option ZL1 appeared in 1969 it was referred to as a "Special L88" with an aluminum block. All the race options were required; however, only two were ordered in cars from the factory: a yellow coupe with a manual transmission and an orange convertible with an automatic. A total of 94 ZL1-spec engines were produced, 80 for manual cars and 14 for automatics, of which 69 went into Camaros. The others were ordered by road and drag racing teams for competition use.

The aluminum-block ZL1 program also had another major roadblock when it came to ordering: The price was astronomical. It cost more than $3,500 more than a standard L88 of which 116 were sold in 1969. The RPO actually cost more than a base convertible at the time. In all likelihood, the cost of the ZL1 package would have gone down in the years to come but when threats of emissions add-ons came and then were implemented in the early 1970s, the high-performance factory engine became obsolete. It was impossible to homologate it into a street car. The first and only year of the ZL1 engine option was 1969.

Today, both ZL1-optioned Corvettes are in the hands of private collectors, and both have been worked on by Corvette Repair. The next best thing to owning a ZL1 Corvette is owning one of the rare engines that could potentially still be out there.

Several years ago, Kevin was offered such an engine by Floridian John Davis. Davis had found the engine in England, where it had been

This factory L88 convertible looks surprisingly unassuming from the front, considering the monster 500-plus horsepower V-8 that powers it. When a customer brought in this white-on-blue convertible, Kevin thought that it might have been the original ZL1 test car, since it fit all the criteria. Unfortunately, it wasn't, and the hunt continues!.

Although the ZL1 option package didn't appear on Corvette order forms until 1969, Zora Arkus-Duntov and his engineering team were developing the potent aluminum-block 427 as early as 1967. As the penultimate GM performance engine of the time, it was featured in several books and magazines upon its release in late 1968. Kevin was offered this one, and after buying it realized it was the same engine used for those promotional purposes. He restored it exactly the way it appears in those publications.

used in a Can-Am car. He knew Kevin was interested in rare big-block Corvettes, and this one was as unique as they come. Based on the serial numbers on all the engine parts and the corresponding work orders that Davis had collected, his engine was the first aluminum-block L88 that was handbuilt in 1967 by Zora Arkus-Duntov and his engineering team. The work orders dated back to August 2, 1967, and it was referred to as a lightweight Mark IV performance engine package. Engineering was also developing higher-flowing prototype cylinder heads at the same time in addition to other engine parts; otherwise, the production versions are nearly identical.

Although many believe that there are other differences between the L88 and ZL1, Kevin's research leads him to believe that the two engines differ only in terms of the aluminum block. They both used an aluminum intake, aluminum heads, same carburetor, and the same oil pan.

Kevin's prototype engine has the special distinction of being used as the cover model for the December 1968 issue of *Hot Rod* magazine. It was also featured on the cover of *How to Hotrod Big-block Chevys*. Kevin wasn't aware of this when he bought the engine until he saw the December 1968 issue of *Hot Rod*. The image is so clear on the cover that you can actually read the casting number right above the water pump. It was the same number as the prototype engine that he had just purchased! And a special engine just got a little more special.

Armed with that magazine cover, Kevin set about restoring the engine to look exactly like the one on the cover, with yellow headers and a bright green fan. After the restoration, he showed the engine at Corvettes at Carlisle, where it was invited to the Chip's Choice area, the NCRS National Convention in Kansas City, and the Muscle Car and Corvette Nationals in Chicago. Everyone who sees it is stunned that it survived over the years, and they love seeing it displayed with the magazine cover, which Kevin had blown up to poster size.

"If you look at the picture carefully, the fan is spinning," he says. "I don't know how they did that because the engine isn't running, so I was thinking about trying to make the fan spin electronically."

Chevrolet built 53 such test engines beginning in 1967, with this particular example most likely finding its way into a white '68 convertible with a blue interior that was used as Arkus-Duntov's personal test mule. Although most test mules were destroyed at the crusher, there's always a chance that they somehow survived.

"What if I could find that car today? Boy, that would be the holy grail of Corvettes," Kevin muses. "An original-engine ZL1, and it would be a preproduction car, which would be cool. I've been collecting a lot of magazines and looking for a white big-block, preferably an L88. We actually had one here and I thought that could be the car, but it wasn't. The car has to be a '68 because it has 1968 doors in the picture and it would have been a test bed for the ZL1, which came out in 1969. The car would have been shipped directly to Engineering. So if I could find a white 1968 L88 convertible with blue interior that went straight to Engineering, there's a possibility it might be the car."

Grand Sport #002 Engine

The original Grand Sport Corvettes, although owned and raced privately, were about as close to factory racing cars as General Motors could make. They were never meant to be street cars; unlike all the other Corvette race cars, they were purpose-built for the track. Even in 1969, the cars six years old at the time, they were still effective at the major racing events. Grand Sport #002, now owned by Fred

The TRACO-built engine in the firm's signature light gray paint flanks the mighty ZL1 display. Unlike the ZL1, the Grand Sport engine is unrestored and sits just as it last competed within the fenderwells of Grand Sport #002.

Simeone in Philidelphia, was for many years owned by Ed Mueller. Mueller was known as having one of the finest Corvette collections on the planet in the 1980s, and was one of Kevin's first customers. In fact, the first car of his that Kevin worked on was his 1969 factory ZL1 yellow coupe.

For his first 17 years of business, Ed Mueller had at least one car being worked on by Corvette Repair, oftentimes two or three. He and Kevin bonded over their love of high-end Corvettes and he taught Kevin much about the world of million-dollar cars. This is the same gentleman who had once called him an ***hole for wasting his talent on small-block high-production cars. In fact, Kevin almost had Mueller's Grand Sport #002 in the shop until he sold it for a $300,000 profit right before sending it in for a restoration.

One day, Mueller called Kevin and told him that he was retiring from the collector car world, which had become like a full-time job to him. His car facility was littered with rare Corvette parts and random engine parts. He invited Kevin to bring his truck and load it up with whatever he wanted; he barely charged him for anything. He just wanted everything gone and he knew Kevin would appreciate it.

As Kevin was hunting around, loading up his truck with all sorts of useful parts, he noticed a complete engine sitting there, half covered. The light gray paint on it immediately signified it as having been built by TRACO, the California-based engine shop used by the best race teams in the country. It had the usual abuse markings of an engine that had seen actual track use and Kevin was stunned to find it sitting there. "What's this?" Kevin asked, curious about the history of the engine and how it came to be there.

"Oh, I forgot about that engine," Mueller replied. "I probably should have given it to the owner of the Grand Sport when he bought it from me. Oh, well, I already gave him the car, so it's yours now. That's the backup engine for Grand Sport #002."

"I can have this engine?" Kevin asked, shaking with excitement at the prospect of owning the built 427 used in one of the most famous and valuable Corvettes in history. Mueller confirmed that Kevin could have the engine, pointing out that there was nothing he could do with it since he didn't have the car anymore. The casting numbers cleared it as having been built in 1969 and the battle scars proved that it had been raced.

Kevin showed the Grand Sport engine next to the ZL1 at the NCRS National Convention along with the CERV II engine that was in his shop at the time. "That engine was a big hit," he says. "I haven't done anything with it. At some point, it would be nice to get it back with Grand Sport #002. I've been very lucky to get these engines, an original Grand Sport engine that raced and an original prototype engineering and development ZL1. And they both just fell into my lap."

CHAPTER 21

1965 Black/Black Tanker

LEGENDARY BARN FIND

Peter Klutt of well-known Legendary Motorcar Company in Halton Hills, Ontario, Canada, had tracked an old Cadillac to a Los Angeles warehouse sometime around 2011. Sitting in the warehouse also happened to be a black mid-year Corvette coupe so, as any car guy would, Klutt went over to inspect it. It had fender flares, a large aftermarket shifter, and a tall rear deck, signaling that this car had not only been raced, but it was a rare Tanker that was likely meant for serious racing right from the factory.

Legendary Motorcar Company was a busy shop at that time. A hit reality show on the Velocity television network featured the shop and Klutt, and he had no room or manpower to take on a restoration of the magnitude that the black Tanker would require. Even so, he knew a great car when he saw one, and bought it on the spot. He knew someone who would be able to give the Corvette the attention it deserved: Kevin Mackay.

Kevin immediately recognized the car as the only black/black 365-hp Tanker he had ever seen out of the total 41 produced in 1965, and the 25 left in existence. Kevin gladly paid his friend for the car, the rarity and factory black paint made for a car he wanted for himself. It was one of the best street mid-years he had ever seen, and being a sucker for black Corvettes, this would be the one he'd restore for himself.

After some time had gone by, and the car sat at Corvette Repair, customer Doug Fortune walked in and immediately fell in love with the car in its grungy, as-found condition. He, too, knew the rarity of the black-on-black Tanker and lusted after it for his own collection. Kevin told him firmly that the car wasn't for sale. It wasn't even a question of money; he wanted that car for himself. A while after that, Fortune was back at Corvette Repair and asked to see the cars in Kevin's garage. He showed him, and once again, he was drawn to the barn-find black Tanker.

"I want that car," Fortune repeated again. "You're never going to have the time to do it for yourself."

"I already told you, Doug, you're not going to get this car. It's not for sale. I'm going to do it eventually. Right now I'm too busy, but one day I'll do it."

Six months later, Kevin received a call from Doug Fortune, asking if he was ready to sell the car. It still wasn't for sale, but Kevin promised that if another Tanker came up, he would be first in line to be able to buy it. "You're never going to find another one like that," Fortune pointed out. He was, in all likelihood, right, but Kevin had a knack for coming across cars that no one ever thought would be

Few things in this world are quite as beautiful as fresh black paint on a Sting Ray coupe. Throw in a set of knockoff wheels and blackwall tires and the package is complete.

found, and that no one had even known about.

A year went by. Fortune was relentless. He asked about the car every time he saw Kevin. The answer was always no. At least, that was until the answer was yes. "One day he came by and he must have caught me at a weak moment. He told me that if I sold him the car he'd give me the restoration right away. I had just hired a new guy, and because I like to keep everyone really busy, I probably wouldn't have the time to do the car for myself. I told Doug that I'd sell it to him for a certain price, and not a penny less, and that he would give me the restoration. He couldn't get the word 'Sold!' out of his mouth fast enough."

Like Kevin, Doug Fortune is a perfectionist. He wants everything done correctly and he wants the awards to prove it. He also likes having a complete history of his cars to add even more credibility. Kevin was concerned about this last part. Because no other black/black Tanker had ever surfaced, he was worried that a perfectly restored one would be difficult to believe. Everything can be faked.

This black/black 1965 Tanker sat in storage for decades before being discovered by Kevin's friend Peter Klutt. This California car had been perfectly preserved over the years since its racing career ended. At the time, it was believed to be the only black/black 365-hp Tanker in existence and needed to be thoroughly vetted before undergoing a complete restoration.

The first step was to introduce the barn find to the public, which they did at Bloomington Gold in 2014. The car was shown exactly the way Peter Klutt had found it in that Southern California warehouse several years before. Corvette experts from all over the country stopped by to inspect the recently released discovery and confirm its authenticity. They did, and it was now known to be a real black/black Tanker.

"It didn't make any difference what condition it was in, it was a real car, and now everyone knows it's a real car," Kevin explains. "We showed it exposed before we restored it because we knew people would question it."

With the car publicly confirmed by independent experts, the Corvette Repair team went to work on the restoration. Because the large fender flares on the car had been so deeply ingrained into the fiberglass, Kevin had to find a new nose and a set of quarter panels to replace those that came with the car. This isn't quite as easy as cutting them out of another mid-year Corvette because 1965 Tanker quarter panels use a unique yellow fiberglass similar to what was used in 1963. Everything after 1964 used grayish fiberglass and if you're going to restore a tanker, it must have yellow fiberglass on the quarter

The aftermarket shifter required that a big opening be cut in the car's center tunnel. The tunnel was easy to fix, but it was extremely lucky that the original transmission and interior were still there.

Although this interior appears to be a total loss, it is actually perfectly preserved under the thick coating of dust and grime. The door panels and dash just needed a good scrubbing. The seats were in good shape and only needed new covers. The big gas tank, fill neck, and special cover only needed cleaning and some minor repairs as part of the concours-level restoration.

panels. Doug was able to source a set from Andy Cannizzo in New Jersey, who's earned himself the nickname "Mr. '63" for his massive collection of 1963 Corvette parts.

The interior of the tanker was dirty as can be, but it was all original except for the Hurst shifter and shift gate that had been cut out of the flooring to make it work. Everything was shabby, but original, and therefore would be reused. The door panels were in beautiful shape and treated to a good soapy scrub to appear brand new on the final product. New carpet and seat covers went in, but luckily, the tank, tank cover, and fill neck were all in good condition. The frame was one of the most rust-free frames Kevin had ever seen on a mid-year Corvette.

When it was halfway restored, bare fiberglass on a rolling chassis, Kevin took a minute to look at it. With all the serial numbers easily visible on the major parts, he thought this would make another great opportunity to have experts inspect the car as well as show off his shop's craftsmanship. He took the partially restored Tanker to the NCRS Boston regional meet, and once again, the experts swarmed, searching for a number or part that was out of place. The car continued to receive praise and, upon completion, it was taken back to Bloomington where many people remembered the car from its previous barn-find condition.

At the Muscle Car and Corvette Nationals in Chicago that year, where the car won a Triple Diamond award, Peter Klutt nearly walked right by it before stopping to turn around. "Wait a minute," he said. "Is this the car we found in California? This can't be the same car."

It was, and Kevin introduced him to the car's new owner. Klutt invited Doug Fortune to be featured on his show talking about the car. Fortune was overjoyed for the honor.

It's hard to tell that this is the same car as the one found in that California garage. This is part of why Kevin believes it's important to keep these special cars in the public eye throughout the restoration process. Although it's hard to believe, these two cars are one and the same, and the proof is right there for everyone to see.

The Reverse Hunt

Unlike the special cars that Kevin seeks out to hunt down, every now and then one comes to him and he has to do a backward search to piece together the car's history. This one was especially interesting because, even though it was obviously raced, it also had a radio, power windows, and a heater, luxury features usually associated with street cars. But it didn't have a roll bar, so it couldn't have raced at all that high of a level. Add to the fact that the shipping and data report revealed that the car's initial dealership was Harry Mann Chevrolet in Los Angeles, a known high-performance shop that brought the distinctive 1960s Southern California style to many of the cars that went out its doors.

Kevin was able to track down who he believed to be the original owner and called him up to learn more about the car that he had purchased in 1965. The owner was confused, saying that he thought he sold it to a guy named Peter. Kevin told him that Peter had sold it to him and that he had sold it to one of his customers named Doug. The original owner was upset, and wanted to know what Kevin paid for the car.

"I didn't want to say the price because I didn't know how he would react," Kevin says. "I told him that the price really wasn't important.

"He said, 'Well, if you're not going to tell me the price, don't ever call me again.' And then he hung up. So I tried calling him back and he didn't pick up his phone. I contacted his sister and she told me that's the way her brother is and she had nothing to tell us."

To try to sway the owner to help with details about the car's early history, Kevin is currently developing a binder full of pictures, documents, information, magazine articles, and awards to send to the owner to show what became of his car. In the meantime, he and Doug Fortune continue to show the car, hoping that someone who sees it remembers it from its early days in California and is able to shed some light on that.

"You never know who you're going meet at a show and that's why I like showing this car. We always find another piece of the puzzle to put together."

CHAPTER 22

1953 Corvette #003

THE WORLD'S OLDEST CORVETTE CHASSIS

General Motors Head of Design Harley J. Earl decided in the early 1950s that the company needed a small, lightweight sports car to compete with the various European road racers on the track and in dealer showrooms. He placed Chevrolet General Manager Ed Cole in charge of what was secretly referred to as "Project Opel" in late 1952.

The First Production Corvette

Production Corvettes began rolling off the Flint, Michigan, assembly line on Tuesday, June 30, 1953. All were painted Polo White and had red interiors and black canvas tops. The first prototype Corvette was introduced to the public at the 1953 New York Auto show as part of GM's Motorama exhibition. It was the first fiberglass-bodied American sports car and the initial public reception made it a major score for General Motors. Even though the car looked destined for the racetrack, its running gear was simply pulled from other Chevrolet models such as the 235-ci 150-hp Blue Flame 6-cylinder engine, solid-axle rear end, 2-speed Powerglide transmission, and drum brakes.

Because the first two Corvettes, #001 and #002, were sent to Engineering for testing and development, the first Corvette sold to the public was #003. However, #003 wasn't destined for public consumption just yet; on July 7, 1953, with 67 miles on the odometer, it was delivered to the GM Development department. Because both previous cars had been handbuilt, General Motors needed to run complete, real-world testing on an actual production car. #003 was given a five-hour shake test at -20 degrees F at the Harrison Radiator facility in Lockport, New York, followed by a 5,000-mile Belgian block strength test. Instead of trashing the first of only 300 Corvettes destined for showrooms in 1953, the car was completely rebuilt with a new frame per Chevrolet Engineering work order #19013-27, which was issued on August 20.

With a new frame supporting it, but retaining its original E53F001003 VIN, #003 continued to serve as a Demonstrator and Design Check car through October 1953, at which point it was delivered and sold in the Los Angeles area. At the same time, cars #001

***Talk about a case of split personalities! From the passenger side, this 1953 looks like a perfect Corvette Repair restoration. From the driver's side, the 1953 shows off its true personality as a Corvette Repair Unique Creation. Everything on the car is perfect, down to the location of the floating headlight and badges. Inset:** It might not look like much, but this frame is labeled with serial number 003, and has been verified as the oldest Corvette chassis in existence and the first to be sold to the public.*

and #002 continued to be used for a variety of generic tests and then reportedly were destroyed.

We know that #001 was destroyed because it was the unfortunate mule of a fire test. Techs stuck a rag in the gas tank and lit it on fire to see how long the fiberglass body would burn and what properties it would display. That was testing and development in 1953. Parts of the #002 car are believed to have survived, and there is currently too much misinformation out there about the car to relay its current state here.

The first production car's history differs little from most other early Corvettes in that it was purchased from a used-car lot in California in 1958 by second owner John Crockett, who then placed it into storage in 1963. It remained in storage, although the title changed hands several times, until 1987 when it was purchased by Les Bieri, Howard Kirsch, and John Amgwert. By then, Corvette had become an American icon and #003 was too important and valuable to waste away in storage.

At that time, the car was given a complete and meticulous restoration with guidance from General Motors, which was completed in May 1990. It toured the country as the oldest Corvette in existence, earning Bloomington Gold, an NCRS Arkus-Duntov Award, and a spot in the Corvette Hall of Fame. #003 was purchased by the Ressler family for their collection at the 2006 Barret-Jackson Scottsdale auction where it hammered for $1 million.

What About #003's Chassis?

Throughout automotive history, far too many incredible vehicles and components have been ordered destroyed following severe testing. Although #003's body continued with the giveaway VIN, the original frame was lost, and thought to have been destroyed. That is until 1977 when Florida attorney Phil Havens separated the body from the frame on his newly acquired 1955 Corvette. He noticed some modifications that wouldn't be present on a factory frame and was worried that someone might have replaced his frame with one from a crashed car.

He was shocked to discover a 1953 VIN on the frame, specifically, serial number E53F001003, in two locations. He first spoke to the police department to find out if there was any funny business, but they cleared the numbers. He then spoke to Sam Folz, president and founding member of the NCRS, who came to Florida to confirm that the frame was original using an acid test. He qualified the frame to be genuine; it definitely came from Corvette #003.

To complete the restoration on his '55, Havens sourced a correct 1955 frame and turned his recently discovered #003 frame into a rolling show piece. He first showed it at the 1983 NCRS meet in Cypress Gardens, Florida. It made the cover of *Vette Vues* magazine at the time and an article was written about it in *Corvette Restorer*.

"I remember that car in the 1970s when they first started talking about it," Kevin Mackay says. "Then the frame just kind of vanished. Then in 2012, I was on eBay, and the frame came up for sale! It was from a guy in Florida, so my first thought was that it was Phil Havens."

Kevin has a client whom he thought would be interested in doing something with the frame, Ed Foss, so he called him and told him about it. He told him that the frame from the world's oldest Corvette just popped up on eBay. Foss was immediately interested. After contacting owner Phil Havens, Foss purchased the frame. Havens stripped the running gear from the frame that he had been using to move it around and shipped it to Corvette Repair. #003 was reintroduced to the public in its as-delivered state at Bloomington Gold that year where it was inducted into the Great Hall.

"In 2014, we showed it at the NCRS National Convention in Kansas City," Kevin says of #003's journey. "We had all the experts look at that bare chassis in unrestored condition. Everyone confirmed that it was definitely the chassis. I had people who wanted to buy it, but Ed said, 'Let's bring it back to life.'"

Foss had quite a few good options ahead of him that the Corvette Repair team could do with his frame. They could turn it into a driveable chassis or just a rolling chassis. They could do a see-through car as they had previously done with a '65. Foss wanted a cutaway car. He said, "I want you to cut the car right in half."

Kevin's only question was, "Which side do you want open, Ed?" He decided on leaving the driver's side open because that's where the serial numbers are located and could be seen easily.

Corvette Repair spent 4,000 man-hours building the special creation, its most daunting one yet. The car is completely functional and driveable, but it's not street legal and is meant for educational purposes only.

As part of the cutaway "restoration," everything on the car had to be date-coded correctly for an early 1953 production car. The engine, transmission, shocks, regulator, and anything else with a number is correct for the VIN number. Many of the country's leading experts on 1953s assisted with the project, supplying parts and information, as this was the first time the shop had done an early 1953. The first 25 cars to roll off the production line used special tester car hubcaps because the 1953 hubcaps weren't ready in time. Kevin found an NOS set still in its GM box.

Owner of the #006 Corvette, Steven Sokoloff, played a tremendous role in helping the team piece together the cutaway car, as did Brett Henderson, who supplied the engine and transmission. Steve Doutzen and Cory Peterson also assisted greatly in the restoration process. "These guys are the best in the hobby. There were things that we were missing, and they either had them or could find them for us."

The team worked around the clock to get the driveable cutaway car finished in time for the 2017 Amelia Island Concours d' Elegance. "We pulled a rabbit out of our hat and got it done," Kevin recalls. "I'm glad it's done; it's a relief on my part. We didn't even know how it was going to come out. We just took our time. There was a lot of engineering, a lot of fabrication, and a lot of cursing, and yelling, and throwing stuff. There was a lot of frustration, but it was all worthwhile. Nobody has ever done what we did."

On the morning of the concours, a crowd had gathered around the transport truck to watch Kevin and his team unload #003. When he got in, started it up, and began driving it, the crowd was floored. "People looked like deer in headlights when I was driving this car. I could feel the eyes on me. Knowing that it's the oldest production chassis in the world, the first car sold to the public, I was driving a piece of history here! I'm so proud of my staff who put this together, working endless nights around the clock.

"The best part is seeing the expressions on people's faces. It's priceless. People walk up and ask, 'What the hell is this?'

"People who saw it thought it was done by Chevrolet and I said, 'No, it was done by Corvette Repair. It was done by my team.'"

After its debut at Amelia, #003 made the rounds at Bloomington Gold, the NCRS National Convention in Texas, and the Concours d'Elegance of America at the Inn at St. Johns. Following the rigorous show circuit, the car is currently displayed in Ed Foss's collection. It's important to note that he and Kevin point out that the display is only of the world's oldest production chassis, and not the body or the rest of the car, which is currently in the Ressler collection in Arizona. Kevin at first tried to work out a deal to get the #003 frame with the rest of the car, but it didn't pan out. The next best thing for the Corvette hobby was to build a showcase for the #003 frame so it could be displayed and enjoyed.

"This project was the pinnacle of all the Corvette Repair special creations that we've done and the most difficult by far. That car almost gave me a heart attack; there were just that many details that needed attention. Everything is operational and functional as it should be. I couldn't even sleep at night thinking about that car. I drove my wife crazy! I'm fortunate to have met the right people over the years and to work on the most important Corvettes ever manufactured by Chevrolet. As long as I've got my health and my senses, I'm going to keep on going."

No detail was left untouched on the cutaway '53 and like Kevin's previous cutaway Corvettes, this one is also completely street legal and 100 percent functional. Notice how the gas cap door is painted but the inner surround is left in natural fiberglass? If you tore apart a '53 Corvette, you'd see the same thing! Although it doesn't look like there's anywhere for the driver to put his feet, there's actually a molded Plexiglas floor there. (Photo Courtesy Bill Erdman)

CHAPTER 23

1966 Steve McQueen Sting Ray L88

AT LEAST ONE MCQUEEN CAR LEFT

Steve McQueen may have made a name for himself on the Silver Screen in films such as *The Great Escape, Bullitt,* and *The Thomas Crown Affair,* but his passion for collecting and driving automobiles and motorcycles is part of what has kept McQueen's legend alive for so long. Sure, he was the original King of Cool, but a big part of that were the cars and motorcycles that he owned, drove around town, rode on racetracks, and even used in many of his films. There is no greater provenance in the collector world to this day than to own a Steve McQueen car or motorcycle. To find a McQueen car or bike that had previously been lost would net some major bucks to the finder!

The *Sports Illustrated* Article

The August 1966 issue of *Sports Illustrated* featured an article written by Steve McQueen in which he tested eight of the latest and greatest sports cars and grand tourers from around the world at Riverside International Raceway in Riverside, California. Although he had an agreement with his movie studio that he wouldn't race anymore, he bent the rules a little bit by going out for a glorified track day. He turned laps around Riverside in a Mercedes 230SL, Cobra 427, Aston Martin DB6, Porsche 911, Alfa Romeo Duetto Spider, Jaguar E-Type, Ferrari 275 GTS, and Corvette. McQueen's favorite car in his test was, not surprisingly, the Ferrari 275 GTS, but the close second surprised everyone, including the King of Cool himself: the Corvette Sting Ray. He wrote, "Other than the Ferrari, it was the best car I drove at Riverside. And let's face it, it went out the door at $5,500 instead of $14,000 . . . . No question, it's a brute, a terribly quick car. It must be one of the fastest production cars you can buy for that kind of money."

The McQueen Corvette

Steve McQueen's test Corvette that day was hardly your average, run-of-the-mill '66 coupe, however. The Milano Maroon coupe was equipped with an L88 427 big-block and M22 close-ratio 4-speed to provide blistering acceleration that McQueen referred to in the article as "turbocharged." The track-ready Corvette had a side-mount exhaust system for that ultimate big-block sound. To make laps quicker and easier, General Motors equipped the car with a Posi-Traction rear axle, J56 special heavy-duty brakes, and F41 special front and rear suspension. For comfort and handling, the car had shoulder belts, headrests (two extremely rare options), teakwood steering wheel, and saddle interior. The car is one of only a handful produced in 1966 with headrests and one of 15 built by May 1966 with shoulder belts.

Steve McQueen brought the L88 Corvette from the* Sports Illustrated *article home to continue his "trial" of the car. Here it is sitting in his driveway with his son Chad, and his mother-in-law, Carmen Salvador. (Photo Courtesy Neile Adams McQueen)

Like many magazine test cars in the muscle car heyday, this one was never intended for public distribution; it was a purpose-built test car. It was pulled directly from the assembly line and shipped to GM's engineering department, where it was tested and tuned by Zora Arkus-Duntov personally. Although the showroom 427-ci 425-hp big-block was good enough for the street, and going up against other American muscle, Steve McQueen was going to be testing the car against the very best that Europe had to offer from the likes of Aston Martin, Ferrari, and Jaguar. This Corvette had to be special, and it was the perfect candidate for a new high-performance race engine that GM's engineering division had been working on, dubbed the L88. So when McQueen remarked at the car's awe-inspiring power, it wasn't a typical 425-horse engine under the hood, it was secretly the L88 engine that went on to power the best Corvette race cars over the next several years. Of course the King of Cool was going to love that Corvette!

"They put a cheater engine in there!" Kevin says. "They upgraded the car, if you know what I mean, with special stuff. They wanted Steve McQueen's name on this car and they wanted him to rave about the car. This was no ordinary 427/425 car and Steve just thought it was a regular stock production car. So when he took this car on the track at Riverside, he was completely overwhelmed. Nobody knew because all of this was top secret behind closed doors."

He loved the car so much, in fact, that he asked Arkus-Duntov if he could keep the car for "a while" with the experimental heads, tires, and wheels. Chevrolet arranged to have the car delivered to McQueen, where it remained in his possession until March 1967 at which time the experimental components were removed and the Corvette was officially sold as a stock 427/425 Corvette.

There are pictures of this car in his driveway sitting next to his Jaguar, Porsche, and Ferrari. After McQueen sold it, the car's provenance was lost.

The Hunt

A small handful of GM employees were involved in the initial L88 program, all of whom were notably passionate about Corvettes and Corvette racing. Dick Guldstrand and Zora Arkus-Duntov stand out as the most well-known, but among the team of engineers and mechanics was Bob McDonald, whom Kevin got to know in the

1990s. McDonald worked for Guldstrand at Dana Chevrolet, a popular high-performance Chevrolet dealership, in the 1960s. Several extremely rare cars, many internationally known, came out of Dana Chevrolet, and Bob McDonald worked on most of them behind the scenes.

"I became really friendly with Bob over the years," Kevin says. "I'd bump into him at the track and we'd talk. He knew all about the L88 program. I always asked him about the L88 stuff to see what he could remember."

On February 15, 2000, Bob and Kevin were having one of their L88 chats when Bob thought to ask, "Kevin, you know that the first year of the L88 was 1967, that was the first year they were sold to the public. But did you know they did a lot of development test L88 cars before 1967?"

Kevin actually had known about the handful of 1966 L88 race cars that General Motors was secretly involved with. Bob continued with his story: "Oh, yeah, they made them in 1965 and 1966. As a matter of fact, one of them went to a very well-known actor. I forget his name. I could tell you the color and that he was really good friends with Zora Arkus-Duntov."

After the conversation, Kevin noted everything Bob had told him about the car, a 1966 Burgundy coupe with knock-off wheels and being owned by a very famous actor. It raced at Willow Springs in 1967 as well. However, a thorough search of every race program from 1967 at Willow Springs turned up nothing.

"The years went by, and I was sitting in a class about the L88 program," Kevin continues. "A guy put a picture up on the screen, and it was a burgundy coupe! I looked into the car, and Steve McQueen was driving! I couldn't believe it, the actor that McDonald told me about was Steve McQueen. He was the number-one actor of that generation. I said to myself, 'I gotta find this car.'"

That's where the hard part begins. Anybody alive at that time who could provide useful information would have to be in their 90s. Kevin started his search online to ascertain as much information as he could about the car from articles and pictures. But he wasn't the only one on the hunt for one of the last unknown McQueen cars.

"I was talking to my friend Franz Estereicher, who's out of Detroit, one day," Kevin says. "And he said, 'What do you know about this burgundy car?'

"I said, 'Don't tell me you're looking for the same car I'm looking for!' He chuckled and told me that he'd known about the car for years. I told him that I just hoped the car was out there somewhere and that if I couldn't find it, I hoped that he could. The next best thing to find a particular car is having your friend find it."

Kevin and Franz talked about the car year after year, with neither finding it, and neither losing his resolve to find it. While in Monterey for the Pebble Beach Concours, Kevin's phone rang. This was the same weekend that he spoke with Chuck Spielman about finding his 1965 Tanker, so the weekend had already been a success in Kevin's eyes. As usual, Kevin picked up after just a few rings to hear his buddy Franz on the other line.

Franz got down to business immediately: "Kevin, I need a big, big favor from you. Remember that Steve McQueen car? I think I found it."

Kevin couldn't believe what he was hearing and asked Franz how he found it. Franz had been searching various Corvette and classic car websites for years looking for maroon/saddle 1966 coupes. The three most important things that needed confirmation were the original VIN tag, the original trim tag, and it had to be an original sidepipe car.

Franz continued: "I already got the deposit on it. I trust you like a brother. Will you go out there and look at the car and tell me if it has these certain things." He read off a list of rare, identifiable characteristics of the car that would likely make it a one-of-one if delivered from the factory in the current trim.

Kevin quickly responded that he would absolutely do that for Franz, and he switched his flight from the red-eye back to JFK airport in New York to Seattle. Luckily, 1966 big-block Corvettes are desirable cars, so Kevin flying in for an inspection wouldn't set off any red flags in the owner's head as it had in the past.

"Through photographs that Franz and I had collected over the years we knew that it was a Milano Maroon coupe with a saddle vinyl interior," Kevin says. "In the pictures from the *Sports Illustrated* article you could also see a headrest seat and side-mounted exhaust system. Of course, it had the big-block. Now, sidepipes are rare, but they're not super rare. It's the headrests and shoulder belts that make the car really unique."

Flight scheduling didn't work in Kevin's favor that day, and he was left with only a 30-minute window to verify the Corvette as being the original Steve McQueen car. He didn't need that much time.

Upon arriving at the warehouse where the car was stashed, Kevin immediately inspected the trim tag. It was the original tag, and sure enough, it checked all the boxes. "Son of a bitch," Kevin said to himself. It was a real sidepipe car, real headrest car, real saddle interior, real big-block, and real Milano Maroon. The car was freshly gone through with a "nice" paint job and a fairly new interior.

Kevin reported back to Franz that this was indeed the car they had been looking for, although it was still just a statistical likelihood and not an outright guarantee. Of the 27,720 cars made that year, only 1,033 had headrest seats. Given that the most common interior color was black, the saddle interior further narrowed that down. Then add in the optional high-performance components including the big-block engine, and the odds were pretty good that this was the car.

Franz proceeded with the sale at Kevin's recommendation and wrote to the NCRS for the car's shipping and data report. Because Steve McQueen lived in Beverly Hills, a Southern California dealership would have improved the likelihood that this was the right car. A dealership in another part of the country would leave more questions than answers.

This car wasn't shipped to a Southern California dealership. The data report came back saying that the car was shipped directly to GM Engineering, the only Corvette to be sent there in that time period, which aligned perfectly with the *Sports Illustrated* Steve McQueen test. There was no doubt that this was the Steve McQueen car that Franz and Kevin had been hunting for. Franz went on to use his contacts at the GM archives to discover correspondence between Zora Arkus-Duntov and Steve McQueen talking about the car in addition to test documents from Engineering.

Supposedly, only 13 development L88 cars were built prior to 1967 with Kevin's Roger Penske racer and the Pedro Rodriguez car among them. It wasn't until 2016 that this most recent one was discovered.

"It's amazing what you find online nowadays," Kevin says. "People really don't know what they have. It's a blessing in disguise that there's just a period-correct engine in the car; otherwise, it could have been identified long ago."

CHAPTER 24

1960 Briggs Cunningham #1

THE LE MANS LAWSUIT HEARD 'ROUND THE CAR WORLD

By Kevin Mackay

I haven't spoken about this since after the lawsuit settlement, and I've never told my side of the story publicly. Here it is.

The Three Cunningham Cars

You know the story already about how I wrote to Le Mans and received the serial numbers from all the Corvettes that raced there. My customer Ed Mueller had a 1967 Sunray DX car that ran at Le Mans. It was the only C2 Corvette that went to Le Mans. So after hearing back from Le Mans, I had the holy grail of the Corvette hobby in my hand: a complete list of serial numbers from every Corvette to race there. I was probably the only guy at the time, in the country, who had that information.

It was amazing that they provided it. I just asked for it by going through the right channels, writing a nice letter, and sending them a bouquet of flowers as a goodwill gesture. I was able to get in there without going over there. Today I don't think you could do it; it's a whole different story. But back then, nobody really cared.

If it weren't for Ed Mueller's 1967 Le Mans scrapbook, I never would've figured it out. So I had those numbers since July 1993 and we were able to get a hit on all three Cunningham cars with the help of some of my customers in law enforcement. I did not get a hit on the Camoradi car, which was the private-entry car, #4. My main focus was the three Cunningham cars. I knew that one car had surfaced already. That car was in California and the last four digits of its VIN were 4117. That confirmed that the owner actually had that car. It had been wrecked in the race in 1960.

So I focused on the #1 car, which is VIN 3535, and the #3 car, which is the class winner, VIN 2538. I got a hit on the #1 car based out of Tampa, Florida, owned by Jerry L. Moore. The other car was owned by James Walsh in St. Louis. I found James Walsh pretty quickly and the rest is history with the #3 car.

But I could not find Jerry L. Moore in Tampa. This is before the computer age for me, so I looked through telephone books and called

Because the #1 car's body was wrecked, the rest of it was likely sold in Briggs Cunningham's home state of Florida and either scrapped for parts or rebodied. In this case, the car was modified with a custom single-headlight body and eventually wound up in storage. Kevin continued to hunt for the car, but the car found him when Rick Carr discovered that the serial number matched one posted online. This photo is of Rick and Kevin with the car as it had been sitting since the 1970s.

operator assistance. I even went to the apartment that he lived in at the time he titled the car and knocked on some doors. I asked the neighbors if they remembered a guy named Jerry L. Moore.

The car was titled under his name in 1974, and by the time I went there in the mid-1990s, I wasn't surprised that no one could remember him. Most people don't live in an apartment building for 20 years. They move around. I didn't find Jerry L. Moore, but I kept looking. Maybe he was still in that area. Every time I went there I asked around, but I had no luck.

Rick Carr Has the #1

In 2012, I was fortunate to be inducted by my peers into the Great Hall of Bloomington Gold. I was selected as one of the top 50 people to be inducted. It's a very prestigious award and they only induct 10 people each year for a period of five years. I was selected by a committee and, from what I've been told, my name had kept coming up. I got the official call from my friend Terry Michaelis, who was on the committee, who congratulated me on my induction. It was a very high honor for me and I was humbled to see all my hard work hunting down and restoring these cars appreciated. It had been a long haul.

I went to the ceremony with my wife, Christina, and her parents and we were hanging out with all my friends in the hobby. It was probably one of the happiest days of my life. Unfortunately, one of my closest friends who had been with me since the beginning, Chip Miller, had passed away in 2004. I thought about my past memories, my ups and my downs, and it was just nice that people recognized all the work that I had done over the years for the Corvette hobby. I just love the hobby and I love the people. I was just floating on air that weekend, excited about getting inducted in the ceremony.

Chip's son, Lance, who I've always been very close with, came up to me and he said, "Kevin, I'm so proud of you. My dad is looking down on you right now. I know he is." It was a very emotional moment for me.

He then told me, "You're not going to believe this. I got a call from a guy named Larry Berman who runs the Cunningham website. He's a historian of old Cunningham stuff. He said he got a call from a guy named Rick Carr in St. Petersburg that he has this old, customized, beat-up Corvette in his dad's warehouse."

It turns out that Rick Carr had to nearly lift the entire body off the car to figure out the year and find the VIN. His father had passed away a couple of years before, and he was going through everything in the warehouse. The car had been heavily customized and had single headlights, so he thought it was a 1953–1957 Corvette. In 1958 and afterward, C1 Corvettes had two headlights on each side, four total.

This car had been so extremely modified that he had no idea what it was. Because the car appeared to be a pre-1958, it should have had the VIN tag in the doorjamb, mounted with two Phillips-head screws; that was the only place he looked. Of course, it wasn't there, as the VIN tag was moved to the steering column in early 1960, where it was securely welded in place.

Over years in storage it had been covered with crud and grime so that even if he looked under the hood, it would be hidden. People had come to look at the car because it was somewhat for sale, and no one could find the VIN. The only place Rick Carr thought he could find a working serial number was on the frame, so he loosened the body bolts, jacked it up with his cousin, and the car was actually a 1960 Corvette with the last four digits 3535.

Rick had previously found some of his father's paperwork indicating that the VIN of the car was S103535 and noted that the car was a 1956. Rick knew that this was not the proper VIN format for 1956, but, because he could not find the VIN on the car itself, he could never confirm it.

Rick Carr's cousin is big into computers, so he did an Internet search for the VIN and found it listed on the Cunningham website, run by Larry Berman. It was listed as the missing #1 Cunningham Le Mans Corvette. Knowing that the car was actually a 1960 Corvette, Carr took a wire wheel to where the VIN tag should be on the steering column, and quickly revealed it. With the frame number and the steering column number matching, he realized that he had found the missing Cunningham Le Mans racer, even though it had been heavily customized.

Larry Berman Enters the Story

Now how did Larry Berman become involved? In the 1990s, when I started tracking down the Cunningham Le Mans cars, I promised Chip Miller that if I ever found the 1960 #3 Le Mans car that I was going to give it to him because it was his all-time favorite car on the planet. I told Chip that as soon as I found the car and bought it, I would give it to him for the same price that I paid for it. He said that if I got him the car, he would give it right back to me and hire me to do the restoration. We shook hands and I said, "I'm going to get the car for you." I didn't really care, I just wanted the car to go to a good home. This was seven years before he passed away in 2004.

Every time we went to a car show, our job was to look at every 1960 Corvette on the show field, in the swap meet, and in the parking lot. Anywhere we saw a '60 Corvette we went up to it and, if the hood was open, we looked on the steering column for 3535. The VIN number can only be on the steering column. If the owner was near the car, we asked if he minded if we looked in the engine compartment. Of course I'd never tell him what I was looking for. We found 3530, 3532, 3551, and we joked and said we were getting closer. Chip and I would laugh and say, "You're not going to believe this, but I found a car that was 3533!" It was really funny and this went on for years, but we never stumbled across car 3535.

We looked for that number for a long time; I had that VIN since 1993. Then Chip started to not feel well and he knew there was something wrong with him. This went on for quite a while and he promised me that he would help me get the #1 car. "In some shape or form," he told me, "I'm going to help you get that car because this has been such an unbelievable experience all these years."

Looking for that #3 car, finding the #3 car, waiting seven years to finally get it from Mr. Walsh, and he said, "I'm going to find that #1 car for you. I'm going to get that car for you. Then we'd be able to show all three cars together. Wouldn't that be an amazing ride and bring so much excitement into the hobby to have all the Le Mans cars and get the three Cunningham cars together for the first time in all these years? It's been 50 years."

I didn't know at the time that Chip had heard of Larry Berman and the Cunningham website and that he gave the VIN number to Larry because he knew he was dying. He knew he had months to live and couldn't look for the car anymore. He was focused on trying to get well. So he went to Larry and said, "Larry, listen to me, I shouldn't be giving this to you, but I'm not going to be around much longer. This VIN was given to me by Kevin Mackay. If you ever come across this number, make sure you tell Kevin or my son about the car. If someone ever calls you or whatever."

Larry always remembered that after he took the VIN number, he put it up on his website. I didn't even know about the website at the time. I wasn't really a big computer person back then. So here it was, 2004, and Chip had given him the number maybe six months before, and I finally hear about the website. I go on to look at it and I see the VIN number. How the hell did Larry get this VIN number? I thought about it. 3535. I can't believe it! I was a little taken back. I thought maybe he did what I did in writing to Le Mans because I had never met the guy and never spoken to him. Maybe he went to Le Mans and with his connections was able to get it. Well, there's nothing I can do about it now; everybody already knows about the VIN number.

But the car still was never found.

In 2012, I was at the ceremony getting dressed and running a little late when I got a call from Lance. He told me that the 1960 Corvette with VIN 3535 was in St. Petersburg, Florida, and that the owner called Larry Berman. Now Lance is a prankster, so I said, "Listen, Lance, this is probably one of the happiest days of my life and now you gotta break my shoes and get me all worked up over this car."

"Kevin, I'm not breaking your shoes. I'm not joking. This guy claims he's got the car."

"Let me tell you something. I don't believe you!"

"Kevin, I'm not fooling around. I'm telling you that this is what I was told. Larry is going to get photographs of the car and he's going to send it to us."

So the ceremony came and of course I was thinking about the car. It had been 19 years since I started hunting for the Cunningham #1 car. Actually I was thinking about that car even longer, but until I had the VIN to confirm the car, I couldn't really hunt for it.

I didn't even know that the car still existed because the #1 car did 32 laps, hit rain, and then went end over end and burst into flames. Maybe the car was destroyed because it crashed and didn't finish the race. It was the first Cunningham car out. That was the car that Briggs Cunningham and Zora Arkus-Duntov were supposed to drive. So I really would love to have gotten that car knowing Arkus-Duntov was supposed to drive it before being pulled out at the last minute. But the fact that Briggs Cunningham himself drove it was pretty cool.

It was a wonderful ceremony and a wonderful experience. It was very emotional, as most of my friends were there. When I got back home and the dust settled, I got back to reality and back to work. I received that email from Lance Miller with pictures of the supposed Le Mans car, which I immediately opened and looked at. Within half

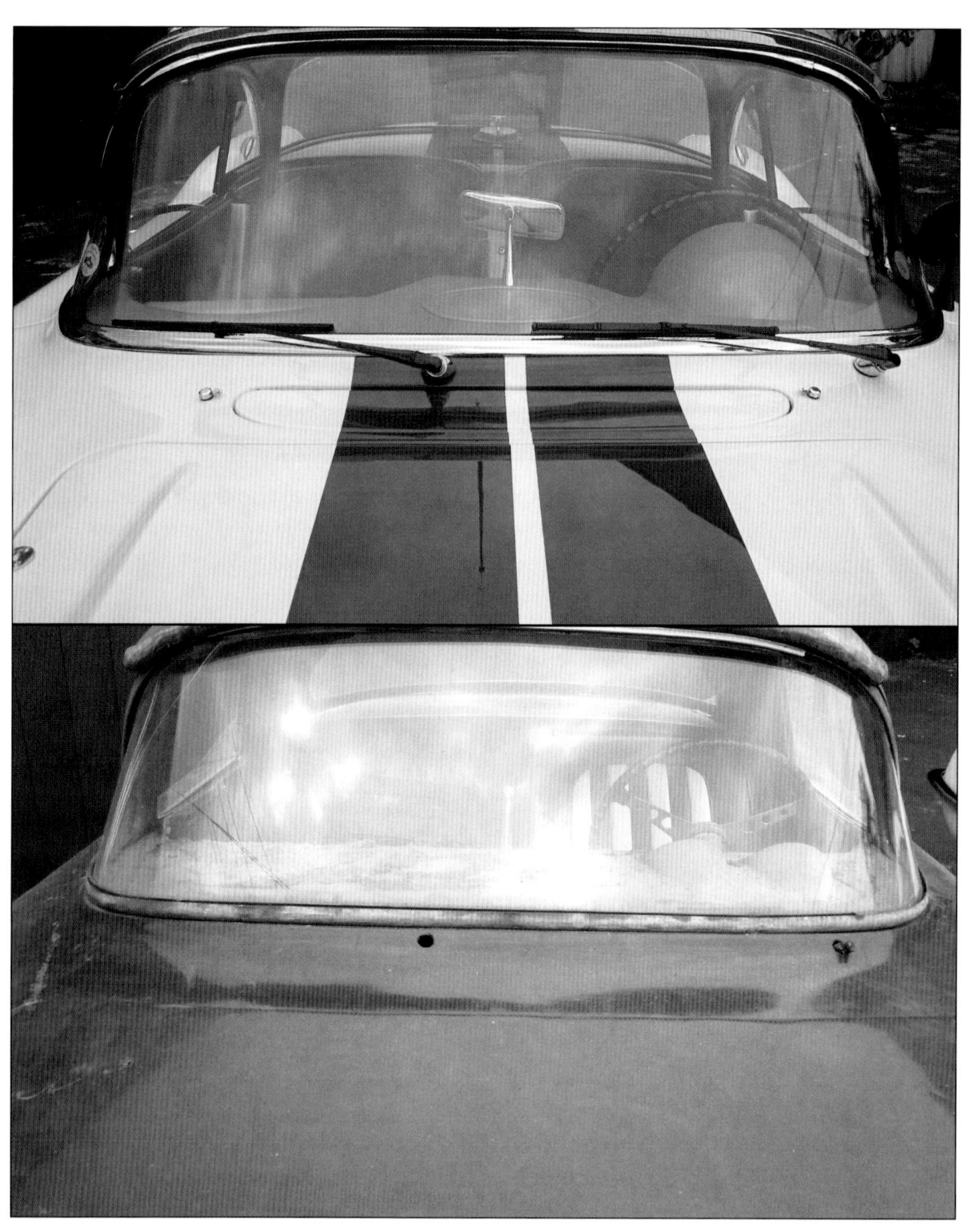

Being one of the only people on the planet to ever work on and spend time with a Cunningham Corvette, since he restored the #3 car years before, Kevin could quickly and easily identify the car as correct. The first thing he noticed was the hole for the wiper arm, which Cunningham modified so that the wipers would go side to side instead of in and out.

a second I knew it was the car. I went over all the photographs and looked at comparisons of forensic evidence.

Cunningham cars were the only cars that moved the passenger-side wiper hole to the center of the body. If you look at any Corvette from 1953 all the way up, the wiper arms are on the outside of the body and they sweep inward. When the car was doing 100-plus mph at Le Mans, I guess the wipers were clashing a little bit, so they took the passenger-side wiper arm and moved it to the center of the body so they would sweep side to side. Back and forth.

As I looked at the picture of the body, I saw that the wiper arms and pivots were missing, but the center hole was there. I knew right there that it can only be a Cunningham car. That was part of the Cunningham trademark. Nobody really knew that because I was one of the few people who had ever worked on a real Cunningham car. When I was working on the #3 car, and I stripped the paint off, the hole was filled because somebody put the wiper assembly back to the stock location. But you can still tell that there was a hole in the center. And on this car, the hole was in the exact same location.

So I called up Lance and I was freaking out. I said, "You son of a gun; it's the car!"

"Well how do you know it's the car?" he asked. "How could you tell?" The car was so extremely customized.

I said, "Look at the damn hole in the middle, right near the windshield. That's for the wiper blade." He agreed. I said, "We gotta make a deal for this car. As a matter of fact, since you've been in touch with Larry Berman and you're much better at computers and writing and everything else than I will ever be, can you help me get this car?"

"Absolutely," he told me. "I remember the story about how my dad was looking hard for you and you got him the #3 car. Now I'm going to get you the #1 car because of my dad. He always talked about the car to me and I know the story very well, Kevin. My dad is still looking out for you; he's looking out for both of us."

The Chip Miller Connection

Chip Miller had submitted the information to Larry Berman, and even though he's not with us anymore, he's still going to help me get that car. If he never gave that VIN number to Larry Berman, the car would be gone forever. If Larry Berman never got that call from Rick Carr, the car would've been lost.

Lance had something in common with Rick because Rick had just lost his dad, too. Because Rick was a car person and into anything with an engine and wheels, I thought this would be perfect for Lance and Rick to start a relationship. Maybe he'd be interested in selling the car. He now knew that it was the Cunningham car, so I just wanted to be fair with him and hoped that he would be fair with us. Lance and Rick began emailing back and forth, and Lance told him that we had an interest in buying the car. The plan was for Lance to buy it from Rick and then sell it to me for what he got it for. That's exactly what I did with his father.

So they were conversing back and forth and Rick knew that the restoration would be very expensive for that car and that he couldn't afford it. A restoration for that car was probably a $300,000 bill at the time, and the last Cunningham car sold for about that at auction. So they came up with a price of $75,000 for the car and Rick was very comfortable with that. So Lance bought the car and I was floating like you wouldn't believe. I was just as excited when I got that car as I was with the Penske car and all the other cars. I said, "I can't believe we found the last missing link. Now we have all the Le Mans cars together, which it was my dream to get them all together and have a big Le Mans reunion."

So I started gathering photographs of the car, and the more photographs I had, the more comparisons I did, and the more I knew that it was the car. So I flew to St. Petersburg and met with Rick and his son. We went to this huge warehouse; he actually had two warehouses filled with all sorts of stuff from his father, who was a criminal court judge. I had a wonderful experience with Rick and his son and I crawled all over the car and the more I looked at that car the happier I became and the more excited I got. He gave me all the information and documents that he had from the car. He told me that his dad saw this ugly Corvette and bought it for $200 in the 1970s.

I asked Rick if anyone else had seen the car in the past couple of years. He told me "Absolutely not." He was the only one responsible for selling this stuff for his stepmother and the car hadn't moved.

We put it on a transporter and took it home.

Lance and I begin talking about debuting the car as part of the pre-restoration ritual to get as many experts to look at it as possible. He suggested Corvettes at Carlisle 2012 and I thought there would be no better place. This was like a whirlwind for me. I had just been inducted into the Great Hall in June 2012 and now here we were planning to debut this car in August. We began to plan a big party to be held at Chip's house, where his widow, Judy, lived and we'd invite all the experts and press. Everything was going perfectly.

In the short interim, we started promoting the event, and word leaked out that the special car being debuted was the Cunningham car that Kevin Mackay had been hunting for.

Dan Mathis Has the Title

A week or two before the event, I received a very disturbing phone call from Dan Mathis, a name I had never heard before. He asked me if I was Kevin Mackay. He said he heard that I had the Le Mans car. I asked him to clarify who he was and he told me that his dad used to own the car and it was actually his car. I was shocked because Rick Carr's family had owned it since the 1970s.

The next thing he told me was that he had a title for the car. I told him that would be impossible, as the last titled owner was Jerry L. Moore. According to Dan Mathis, Jerry L. Moore had sold the car to his father, Dan Mathis Sr. But even still, Dan Mathis Sr.'s name was nowhere on the title, so I told him I didn't know what he was talking about.

"Well, that car's owned by me now," Mathis told me. "The car was stolen from my dad's house."

"The car was stolen, but you have a title?" I asked him. He suggested that maybe there was something that could be worked out. He told me that I had to pay him because he had a title.

"What are you talking about? I bought this car free and clear on a bill of sale. How can you have a title? The car was under Jerry L. Moore's name. Look, I don't know what kind of a joke this is, but this is my car."

I was all confused, so I called Lance. He had no idea what it was about. So then I called one of my law enforcement friends and asked him to run the VIN. The last time we ran the VIN, it showed up as titled to Jerry L. Moore. And the car hadn't changed owners or seen the light of day since then.

Sure enough, my friend told me that the car had been titled in Tampa two days earlier by Dan Mathis. I had already had the car three weeks at this point. How could this guy get a title to a car that was gone? I knew something was going on here, but I didn't understand it. I was just blown away.

I took the car to the party, which was a wonderful event. I showed it just the way it came out of the warehouse, filthy dirty, because I wanted to give the car credibility. I had just about every single part for that car ready to restore it because I was hoping that if I ever found the #1 car, I'd have all the parts made already.

The cost wasn't that much to make a duplicate part because I had to get parts made for the #3 car. Every time I had to make a special part, I'd have a duplicate made. I had a dash, exhaust, special Ferrari louvers, hood pins; it was all there and it didn't add that much to the cost to produce two instead of one.

I collected the Halibrand wheels and correct tires. I found the special shocks and fuel pumps, the special material for the seats and doors. I had it all sitting there in case I ever found the #1 car. So not only was I halfway there but I was probably about three quarters of the way there because all the hard stuff was done.

I Had the Bill of Sale

At the party, Lance signed over the bill of sale to me. It was official now: I owned the #1 Cunningham Le Mans car. But something didn't feel right, and I always trust my gut. I said I couldn't debut the car to the public, which was supposed to be done the day after the party. The next morning, I received a call from an attorney claiming to represent Dan Mathis. He told me that they had the title to the car and that I had to release the car to the owner. I knew something was brewing and I quickly took the car home without debuting it. I was sick over that. What the hell were these guys trying to pull?

Then Lance received a call from a *New York Times* writer he knew. He asked what was going on with the car and that a guy was claiming he had the title. Lance filled him in on what had happened and I got back into the research. On the Monday after Corvettes at Carlisle, I received a call from an attorney named Bryan Shook from Harrisburg, Pennsylvania, a friend of the Miller family. He had heard what happened with the car and how it was pulled from its public debut. He became my guardian angel. He said, "Mr. Mackay, I think I can help you. Let's file a lawsuit against these guys."

Having returned from Carlisle with the car, I placed it in a private garage down the block from my shop. I thought things were about to get ugly. Bryan and I worked on the lawsuit all day Monday and all night Monday night. Bryan literally worked more than 24 hours straight for me. We filed suit on that Tuesday afternoon. Jerry Moore and Dan Mathis Sr. worked at a pool company together when Jerry sold the car to Mathis, who never titled the car. So, we filed suit in Pennsylvania, and they filed a federal suit. I would be ready.

Digging into the Backstory

Knowing now that Jerry L. Moore was alive and well, I went back to hunting him down. I flew to the Tampa area to try to find him. I didn't know what to expect with Jerry L. Moore. Here was a guy that I've been looking for for 20-plus years and now I know he's alive and well. I had to find out his side of the story.

I went to the trailer park and started knocking on doors, looking for Jerry L. Moore. One guy pointed out his trailer to me. I knocked on his door while I was on the phone with my attorney, Bryan Shook. I told Bryan that if he didn't hear from me in 30 minutes to call the cops. A woman answered the door and I introduced myself as Kevin Mackay.

"Oh, I know who you are," she said. "You're the guy with the Corvette. Oh, my boyfriend wants to talk to you. He's at work, but you stay right here and don't move." She had two pit bulls in the house, so I told her I'd wait outside. Jerry called while I was waiting. He told me that he was on his way home and that he felt uncomfortable with what was going on. He thought that he might have been scammed.

Jerry L. Moore came home, took me into his trailer, and we sat down and he told me the story.

So I continued digging. I first had to make sure that Jerry L. Moore was legit. He hadn't seen the car since he sold it, so I asked him to describe it to me. At the time, there were no pictures online of the car. He told me exactly what the car looked like in the pictures I had, except that it was Canary Yellow when he owned it.

He remembered the little vent on the hardtop and he described the custom body on it, with two headlights, when he bought it from Mr. B's Paint and Body Shop. "All the work had been done there," he said. I then pulled out a picture of the car and he recognized it immediately. He pointed to the little vent on the hardtop and said there was no doubt that it was the car.

My next step was to find the owner of the auto body shop that did the work. So I went to the library to go through old advertisements and books and everything else. I found a listing in an old Tampa general telephone directory for Mr. B's Paint and Body Shop. I wrote down the address and went there, but the business was long gone.

I started making calls and someone told me that the owner had died in 1972 at 34 years old from testicular cancer. It turned out that was why he sold the car. The guy I spoke to actually had been offered the car before Jerry, but he thought it was so ugly and beat up that he didn't want it. He also remembered seeing the car on a used-car lot at a gas station where it sat for a year before being purchased.

I asked him about Dan Mathis, who he also happened to know because he had Mathis install a concrete patio at his house. He remembered Mathis trading the car to a guy they called "Billy Sunoco" for a Dodge Demon race car.

Next, I tracked down Billy. I found his father, John Lehmkuhle, a Sunoco gas station owner, who said that his son owned the car. I talked to Billy, and he said that he sold the car to a criminal court judge for $200.

While all this was going on, Rick Carr found the original bill of sale to the car listing it as having been purchased in 1976 for $200 from John William Lehmkuhle. The pieces of the puzzle were coming together and the puzzle was getting a little bigger. Billy Lehmkuhle said that Dan Mathis Sr. (a black man) was heavily into drag racing, as was his older brother, Roosevelt. Dan raced a Vega and a Camaro.

Billy told me that Mathis really wanted a race-ready Duster that was sitting on his lot, but he had no intention of selling. So Mathis offered Billy the Corvette, which he accepted, and it sat on his lot at the corner of West Kennedy and Lois Streets in Tampa for a year before Judge Carr bought it and had a friend paint it brown.

Poking Holes in the Story

The battle began, and I'd dug up so much history about what they did and what actually happened. I found Roosevelt Mathis, who lived in Georgia, just over the Florida border. He told me his whole story about drag racing with his brother, Dan, who he lived with at the time. I asked him about the Corvette, but he couldn't remember the car or that anything was supposedly stolen out of the driveway of the house where he lived.

Next, I found the racetrack where they used to run, and even though it had gone out of business, I found the owner. He remembered Dan Mathis drag racing, but he didn't remember a Corvette.

Back then, there were only a handful of black men who were drag racers, and one of them racing a Corvette would have stood out. The owner only remembered Mathis's Vega and Camaro.

What I think happened is that Dan got the car but realized it would be too expensive to put on the track. So he flipped it and took the Duster, which was already prepped for drag racing and just needed an engine. Mathis Jr. claims that the car was drag raced, but it was impossible. I had the 1974–1976 rule books for drag racing that listed the required provisions for racing a car. Fiberglass race cars had to have a metal firewall between the driver and the engine. This car doesn't have that. You couldn't have a gas tank inside the car, it had to be in the trunk and surrounded by aluminum. This car didn't have that. And since Mathis never had the car titled, it couldn't have been on the street. He may have had the Corvette, but it would only have been for a few days.

Another issue is that they claimed the car was stolen from the driveway. I went to two police departments in the area searching for a police report. There wasn't any. There wasn't even a record in the logbooks of anyone calling to report a stolen Corvette. So I went to the old neighborhood where Dan Mathis Sr. had lived and spoke with his old neighbors. They remember Dan having a mid-1970s Corvette, but not an early one. They remember boats and other drag cars, but not the one that I showed them.

I checked Dan Mathis Sr.'s Estate with all his belongings listed, and there's no record of anything related to a Corvette. I even found some of his girlfriends, yet still no one who remembered the Corvette.

Author's Note

As this book was in its final editing stages, the threat of another lawsuit reared its ugly head over the Cunningham #1 car. Because of this, we've chosen to omit the information regarding the first lawsuit and those involved.